For Kelly, Juliette and Oona.
Thanks for all the love.

In loving memory of
Patty and Don

Gratitude

"Hey Jeff, why a book?"

I'm pretty certain the Internet will blow up soon, and with that, millions upon million of nonsense-filled webpages and countless gigs of nut-punching videos will be lost forever. Sad, but it's inevitable.

That's why I gathered up some of my favorite musings from our website, UsedWigs.com, and put them in book form. They shall be preserved for the future generation of belligerent, ferocious apes who will one day enslave all humans and rule the earth... and learn to read. In that exact order. So, that's why this book is staring you in the face. It's for the apes.

Bonus reason: If you ever wanted to take UsedWigs to the bathroom with you (many have inquired how), well, kids, here's your chance.

"Anyone you'd like to thanks?"

I certainly would and will. I'd like to thank Team UsedWigs: Kelly Andrews (book editor), Scott Shrake (web editor and columnist), Russ Starke and Todd Marrone (podcast team, writers). I love these insanely creative and talented people very much and one day hope to pay them.

I'd also like to give some love to all the contributors, past and present, who filled our website with quality workday distractions: Amy Grimm, Charlie Pasquine, Zank McManus, Brian Seymour, Mike Pierantozzi, Dave Barrosse, Kevin Downey, Jr., Dave Hill and some other funny bastards whose names escape me.

Lastly, thanks to Michele Melcher for the lovely cover art and Chris Rugen for the design advice.

Hugs, Jeff

Hi, My Name is Jeff and I Sometimes Smell Like Poop

As I was standing in line at Ritz Photo waiting to get some pictures developed, I noticed no one was in a big rush to assist me. (Yes, I actually get prints of my photos made unlike you, who only has digital versions, soon to be lost forever the next time a Windows update wipes out your hard drive.)

In addition to the aloof staff, the customers in the store gave me a particularly wide berth in the queue.

When one of the slow-stepping employees finally did give me some attention, he was very quick to shoo me away after taking my order. Oh well, not everyone enjoys my company (just ask any of my old cell mates), and I can deal with that. But after another not-so-pleasant encounter at the Super Fresh, where the checkout gal also gave me an odd look of disgust, did I realize there might be something wrong with my physical presentation.

Shower? Check. Deodorant? Check. Spritz of Drakkar Noir? Check. Fly zipped? Check. Teeth brushed? Well, no. But come on, I'm not some obsessive-compulsive clean freak. Anyway, that was not the source of the people-repelling problem.

Only upon return to my house when I was emptying my pockets of some crumpled Washingtons, a dead cell phone, a pitless grape stem and my lucky laminated photo of Zbigniew Brzezinski, did I notice that something extra was also sitting snuggly against my thigh. I pulled this weighty surprise from down deep in my cargo shorts pocket and was shocked to discover it was a plump and mushy clear plastic bag of poop.

Now that you are done gasping, I will answer the question, "Hey stinky, what the hell were you doing with crap in your pants?" Despite having 20/20 vision, bionic hearing and the angelic voice of a master castrato, I am a tad flawed in one key sensory area.

I have absolutely no sense of smell.

Yup, feel free to blast a fart in my general direction and I will do nothing but titter at the always-funny sound. Kiss me hard and long after a garlic and onion pizza and I will pay you your 20 spot, just as we negotiated on the curb — no problem, no need for a mint.

Back to the poop problem: In my defense, the poop was not my own, nor was it the human variety. It was my dog's morning droppings.

You see, some mornings when I take him on his walk we encounter other dogs that like to run up to him and say hello. This does not make my special-needs mixed-breed very happy (especially if he in on his leash) and he tends to go a little crazy. So I need both hands to pick the 25 pounds of frantic fur, hold off the other pup and run away like a spastic fool. In this particular instance, I quickly stashed the bag of poop in my pocket and completely forgot it was there.

This seems to happen at least once a month and usually no one is any the wiser that I smell exactly like Ashlee Simpson's songs sound. For example, one dark day last winter, my lovely wife gave me the brush off after I cozied up to her on the couch to watch some movie trailers on my laptop. Usually this is very important quality time together that we both enjoy. After a minute or so of couch-based snuggling, she politely arose and left without mentioning the stench emanating from her extremely disgusting mate. I believe she immediately hopped in the shower and gave herself a good *Silkwood*-style cleansing.

About two hours later (now 3 pm) I dug my hands into my old hooded St. Joe's sweatshirt pocket (Yes, I went to Catholic school, but only for 16 years) and found a large plastic bag of my pup's poop which was expelled from his furry little body about 8 hours earlier. Wow, I know, that's a lot of time to marinate.

I have a fairly large nose and you would think this prominent proboscis would actually perform its rightful bodily duty and sniff out some nonsense for me.

"Hey Jeff, do you smell smoke?"

"Nope. Relax Woodsy Owl, we're camping in a California forest on super hot, dry day. What could possibly go wrong?"

"Hey Jeff, do you smell gasoline?"

"Couldn't tell ya. Let's just light these M-80s and chat about it later!"

"Hey Jeff, do you smell what The Rock is cookin'?"

"No... no I don't (sob)."

"How about teen spirit?"

"Nothing... I got absolutely nothing (sob sob)."

My beak just takes up valuable facial real estate and does nothing but collect and disperse mucus and occasionally allows a few unsightly nose hairs to peek out for the world to enjoy.

So please help a brother out. If you see me walking down the street with cartoon stink lines hovering around my body and children, rats and dung beetles crossing streets to avoid me, just walk right up, and tell me I'm full of shit.

Business News

Boy Genius Finishes College at 10, Stuck in Crappy Job at 11

Mozart wrote his first concerto at age five. Tiger Woods learned to play golf at three. And now Madison, New Jersey's own child prodigy Jason Pavlick is stuck in a crappy job at age 11.

Under the home-school guidance of his mother, Pavlick finished high school at the age of six. He then breezed through college by the time he was eight and capped off his accelerated education by receiving his MBA from Villanova University at the tender age of 10. Now the precocious young man is a first-year consultant with a financial consulting firm making 58K a year, working 70-hour weeks and hating every minute of it.

"I never really thought about what I wanted to do after my schooling," said a visibly tired Pavlick as he unclips his necktie and downs chocolate milk at McSorley's Pub in Manhattan, where he and some of his colleagues meet for the occasional drink after work.

"I was always good at math, so my parents told me to study finance like Warren Buffett. Great! So here I am, a working stiff busting my ass in low-level financial advisory hell, counseling old biddies about whether to buy 10 shares of this mutual fund or that one, all in a futile attempt to make partner by 15."

With his education complete and a ton of student loans hanging over his head, Pavlick had no choice but to enter the workforce. "I kind of wanted to kick around for a while, you know, have some 'me' time... maybe backpack through Euro Disney for a few weeks."

That didn't pan out. Pavlick was recruited right out of school. "I thought he was a midget when we first met, which actually helped him," said company recruiter Sheldon Goldfarb. "We provide equal opportunity for the differently sized here. I realized I was wrong about Pavlick after he interrupted my interview questions repeatedly to show me some 'high scores' on his Gameboy."

Pavlick said his parents were "banking on People Magazine or one of those stupid 20/20 shows to pick up my story when I was in high school so I could get some scholarship offers. They wrote letters and sent in videos of me playing my mini violin and building robots, but no one was biting. It seems there's a bunch of genius kids like me whipping through mid-level colleges."

The young consultant perked up for moment as he fondly recalled his college days. "I really miss Nova. We just kicked it at the frat house all day. We played video games 24/7 and jammed to Dave Matthews. It was totally chill! I could actually palm the basketball in the frat house Pop-a-Shot games."

But his voice quickly returned to its joyless monotone as he thought to the future, "Now, I got 60 years of crunching numbers and drinking bad coffee at client sites to look forward to. Whoopde-frickin-do. Look at these bags under my eyes... Christ almighty."

Pavlick lives at home with his parents in Madison for the time being. "I'm saving up to build a super cool tree fort."

When Pavlick does have time to hang out with friends in his neighborhood, he is usually teased about being different (he only wears sensible golf clothes and loafers) and his recent weight gain. "Yeah, guess I got a bit of a gut now, but hey, I work so much I just don't have time to hit the swings like I used to."

Listless Effort

Holiday Shopping Tips

* Do not charge anything you can't pay off in the next 23 years.

* *Leatherheads* and *Speed Racer* action figures now 70% off at Rite-Aid.

* McCain/Palin lawn signs make great gag gift wrapping paper.

* Take advantage of that big sale at The Dollar Store.

* The stockings will be filled with disappointment if you shop at J Crew for your Twilight-loving little vamps.

* Remember, the economic crisis is hurting the retailers too, so keep your shoplifting to a minimum.

* Keep receipt for hassle-free return of expensive cocktail dress you really didn't like but still wore to the office holiday party (and on four other occasions).

* Dr. Phil's latest diet book is the perfect gift for your friends who are both fat and dumb.

* Beware: "What are you wearing right now?" is not a standard question when ordering gifts over the phone.

* People love getting cash! Not that worthless American kind, try euros or whatever they use in Canada.

* New "Somali Pirate Ship" Lego set selling fast, get yours soon.

* If Santa's lap is moist, grab your child and skedaddle.

* Buying products advertised in unsolicited emails is a great way to save money and enlarge your penis.

* Doing all of your shopping on Christmas Eve guarantees your loved ones will be receiving the freshest bags of grapes possible.

* Gas stations would not sell neckties if they weren't really great gifts.

* Telling your loved one, "I got you an XXX-Large just to be safe," is not always appreciated.

* Parking can be crazy. To protect your SUV from dings and scrapes, take up at least two spaces with your vehicle. People will leave it alone and definitely won't key it.

* Covering yourself from head to toe in thick mucus is an effective way to discourage pickpockets.

* Mall shopping can be physically exhausting, be sure to bring along your personal trainer.

* Spice things up for the office Pollyanna and burn latest celebutard sex tape on a DVD.

- *Additional reporting by Scott Shrake.*

Pop Culture

Chinese Youths Crazy for English Alphabet Tattoos

"The guy at the tattoo shop told me this means brave and proud warrior in English," said beaming Beijing teenager Hao Tsang as he pointed to the letters GARF freshly inked onto his left bicep. "It's perfect for me because I am very bold and confident, yet spiritual."

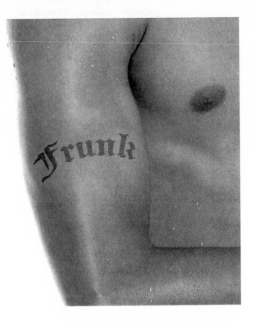

Tsang's friend Yuan Chi Hao also went under the needle for some English language characters. "Mine simply says 'Frunk.' The letters are so beautiful and flow so smoothly into each other. The word actually means 'old soul with young spirit' in English. How cool is that?"

Apparently, very cool.

Throngs of Chinese youths are flocking to tattoo parlors looking to colorfully emboss their bodies with "meaningful" English language words.

"I couldn't decide between CRYMPH or DLECH," said Chengdu high school student Mingmei Lee. "I know they both mean 'beautiful flower dancing in the wind' in American, but I can't decide what looks prettier."

This strange trend mirrors a popular body art movement in the US where many Americans — especially professional basketball players and young celebrities — get Chinese language characters tattooed on their bodies. Many believe the Chinese characters add an air of spirituality to their beings and help present them as enlightened individuals who respect and admire foreign cultures.

Former boy-band member Chris Kirkpatrick proudly displayed his fresh ink after leaving a popular LA tattoo parlor. "Check it out," said the very excited singer as he pointed to the characters on his left forearm. "My man just hooked me up with some mad Asian ink! He says it means 'wise wolf that guards the pack.' That's totally me dawg... I take care of my boys. Cool dat!"

Upon further investigation, the characters were found to actually mean 'dog ass.'

"Listen, these Hollywood hotshots come in here every night wanting something foreign and deep. I only know how to do about twenty Chinese characters, and I have no idea what they mean. But who the hell cares? They just look neat. I make up meanings like 'precious gem floating in pond.' Dumb chicks hopped up on ex really go for that one," said burly ex-marine tattoo artist Jake McNaughton with a hearty laugh.

Beijing tattoo artist Johnny Chang echoed the sentiments of his American counterpart, "Kids are stupid. Funny nonsense tattoos make me laugh ha ha. I take letters from American soda cans and candy wrappers and rearrange them into words. GWIPO is my number one favorite. TWARP is also pretty lucky good!"

Listless Effort

Post-Holiday Office Chat Protocol

1. Approach coworker in cubicle, office or common area.

2. Ask coworker how his/her Memorial Day/Thanksgiving/New Year's/Diwali was.

3. As soon as he/she opens mouth to respond, interrupt immediately and relate in excruciating detail every single thing you did from Friday afternoon to Monday night without taking a breath.

4. Leave. Approach new coworker. Repeat.

Listless Effort

Useful Noncommittal Responses

Why offend when confronted with people's questionable taste? Just answer politely with the following meaningless responses.

Situation: A coworker goes on and on about a lame place they visited.

Response: "I can totally see you having fun there."

Situation: A friend tells you about a horrible band he just loves.

Response: "I hear they have many fans."

Situation: You are served horrible food at a friend's house.

Response: "I can tell this is homemade."

Situation: Someone gushes about a lame TV show or movie.

Response: "That's so right up your alley."

Situation: A woman friend asks your opinion on her god-awful outfit.

Response: "I bet you'll get a lot of wear out of that."

Situation: The viewing of a less-than-attractive newborn.

Response: "Wow, what a baby!"

Situation: A buddy asks what you think about his new ugly girlfriend.

Response: "Dude, she seems really into you."

Situation: A gal pal asks what you think about her new ugly boyfriend.

Response: "He seems like the type who won't cheat."

Situation: You discover your boyfriend is small in the pants.

Response: "It's the perfect size."

Situation: A good friend shows you his cheesy website.

Response: "I don't know which animation to look at first!"

Situation: A guy at a party boasts about his boring job.

Response: "Holy cow, I could never do what you do!"

Situation: A friend gabs about her upcoming wedding for months on end.

Response: "I cannot wait 'til you get married. We're all counting the days."

Situation: An acquaintance asks what you think about her new hair style.

Response: "You know, not everyone can pull that off."

There's a Good Chance Your Friend's Cat Sat on Your Food

If Trish Burns is your friend and you spent last Saturday night eating dinner at her house, there is a very good chance her cat "Smitten" sat on your food. Or licked it. Or walked through it, dipping her litter-soaked paws in the various dishes with each delicate step.

Trish has never trained her cat properly and the kitchen table is definitely NOT off limits to this curious feline. In fact, Smitten loves to jump on the table and sniff about (usually when no one is looking), checking out the latest food additions to her favorite perch.

It probably would have been a good idea if Trish covered the various dishes of food she put out for her buffet-style dinner. But she didn't. She filled the crowded table with a lasagna, ham, potato salad, Caesar salad, broccoli and asparagus at 6:30 pm. Her guests didn't enter the kitchen until 7:30 pm. This gave Smitten a full hour to enjoy "first dibs."

Without a Trace

Smitten's dainty little paws and butt leave little, if any, trace of her furry, flea-filled touch. Her sticky little tongue (which spent most of the afternoon in her anus) produces a very small quantity of saliva. So you probably didn't even notice that Smitten licked your chicken about 20 times.

Luckily, most people at the party were pretty buzzed (especially Mike, he had like six vodka and tonics before he got there) and didn't discern any cat-flavoring in the food. Jane however, did take note of a couple of gray hairs sticking to a piece of ham, but she didn't say anything because Trish worked so hard making all the food. She didn't want to upset her.

Free Band Names!

We think up band names all the time (mostly silly, some actually usable) and have been posting them on our site for many a year. Here's a bunch of gems that our readers have taken for their very own. Need a name, rockstar? We still got a gaggle of fabulous free monikers. Get a good one: *www.usedwigs.com/free-band-names/*

♦ **Ripen with Rage** - taken by a five-person black metal band from NY.

♦ **Perfect Attendants** - taken by emo/punk band from Portland, OR.

♦ **The Thai Rants** - taken by an emo punk three-girl band from the UK.

♦ **{AwkwardHug}** - taken by Moose.

♦ **Can You Fear Me Now?** - taken by an emo hardcore band from OK.

♦ **Punctured Petrol Tanks** – taken by a four-piece punk band from AZ.

♦ **Rag Arm** - taken by a emo/ alternative/indie/punk from Montana.

♦ **Plans for Dinner** - taken by seven-piece ska band from NJ.

♦ **A Judo, A Chop Chop!** - taken by a hardcore band from Alabama.

♦ **Peaceably Possible** - taken by a alternative rock band from Texas.

♦ **The Blistereens** - taken by garage band from Rochester, NY.

♦ **Better Let Her** - taken by an alternative rock band from WI.

♦ **Orthodoxsiders** - taken by a four-girl rock band from Iowa.

♦ **The Ferntickles** - taken by a country/Christian rock band from IL.

(More names peppered throughout the book!)

Rapper Shows Off His Two Affordable and Practical Vehicles on "MTV Cribs"

MTV abruptly halted filming of the latest episode of "Cribs" yesterday, and plans to scrap the entire segment that featured a tour of platinum-selling rapper P-Krunk's mansion in suburban Atlanta.

Producers said the show was going well until they were led outside to check out his fleet of presumably tricked-out rides. "We were shocked, and dare I say appalled, when P-Krunk opened up his garage door and exposed two non-customized, frequently driven vehicles showing a bit of wear and tear: a 1998 Ford Windstar minivan and a 2005 Toyota Corolla."

Unfazed by the producers' grimaces and gasps of disappointment and confusion, P-Krunk began a detailed tour and description of his average autos.

"Check it dawg, my minivan is mad sensible. It gets crazy gas mileage and it's hella roomy, yo. I'm big pimpin' when I load up my shorties and my crew and we kick it at the Mickey D's drive-thru," said the married, 28-year-old father of two. "Gotsta have the removable back seat too, so me and my boo can be loading up bags of garden mulch and manure at Home Depot."

The rapper carefully wiped down the exterior of his minivan — gently cleaning some dirt off the "My Child Is an Honor Student at Peach Tree Prep" bumper sticker — with a chamois and moved on to his "main ride."

"You feeling my Corolla?" P-Krunk queried as he relaxed in the cloth-covered driver's seat of the moderately priced, four-door, gray family sedan and played with the small plastic knobs of his factory-installed AM/FM radio with cassette and single CD player. "I like my B.Seigs & Freeway playing at a low, pleasant volume so I can pay attention to the roadeezy fo' sheezy." The bass was definitely not humping his face as the tinny hip-hop songs barely trickled out of the two standard three-inch speakers mounted in the gray plastic dashboard.

When a cameraman pointed out that the car was missing a hubcap, the rapper laughed and said, "No big thang, nothing a twenty-spot can't fix down at the junkyard."

Asked if he plans on buying more expensive performance cars or a giant Hummer like many of his newly rich contemporaries in the near future, P-Krunk quickly responded, "Ten grand for rims? No my brother, this baller is hanging on to his paper. I don't need to be rollin' on dubs to represent and I sho' as shizzle don't plan on being a broke-ass bitch this time next year. Who do I look like, Hammer?"

"Cribs" segment producer Jonah Rothelsberg explained the reasoning behind shelving the show. "I appreciate P-Krunk's unique taste, but we have a responsibility to our young viewers and advertisers to show the real lifestyles that are true to the artist's genre of music. A rapper who doesn't capriciously spend all his money on cars and 100-inch plasmas is an anomaly that strains credibility. Our viewers would think we made this up or were trying to punk them." Rothelsberg cleared his throat and continued with a grin in a fake urban patois, "Sorry playa, my homies just ain't havin' it."

Listless Effort

Old School!
Too Old to Play Teens

The Mathletes Club here at UsedWigs High have compiled a classroom full of actors who were well past their teenage years when they portrayed high-schoolers on the big and small screens. Age calculations are based on when the film was released or the year the character debuted on the TV show. The information was gleaned from IMDB.com.

ACTOR	BORN	FILM/TV SHOW	YEAR	AGE
Stockard Channing	1944	*Grease*	1978	34
Curtis Armstrong	1953	*Better Off Dead*	1985	32
Sean Patrick Thomas	1970	*Save the Last Dance*	2001	31
Olivia Newton-John	1948	*Grease*	1978	30
John Cho	1972	*Better Luck Tomorrow*	2002	30
Derek Luke	1974	*Friday Night Lights*	2004	30
Alan Ruck	1956	*Ferris Bueller's Day Off*	1986	30
Frank Whaley	1963	*Swing Kids*	1993	30
Stacey Dash	1966	*Clueless*	1995	29
Gabrielle Carteris	1961	*Beverly Hills, 90210*	1990	29
Ron Lester	1970	*Varsity Blues*	1999	29
Gedde Watanabe	1955	*Sixteen Candles*	1984	29
Parry Chen	1973	*Better Luck Tomorrow*	2002	29
P.J. Soles	1950	*Rock 'n' Roll High School*	1979	29
Tony Danza	1951	*The Hollywood Knights*	1980	29
Glynn Turman	1946	*Cooley High*	1975	29
Kerr Smith	1972	*Final Destination*	2000	28

ACTOR	BORN	FILM/TV SHOW	YEAR	AGE
Adrian Zmed	1954	*Grease 2*	1982	28
Gabrielle Union	1972	Bring It On	2000	28
Jeff Conaway	1950	*Grease*	1978	28
Antwon Tanner	1975	*One Tree Hill*	2003	28
Jon Heder	1977	*Napoleon Dynamite*	2004	27
Parminder Nagra	1975	*Bend It Like Beckham*	2002	27
Selma Blair	1972	*Cruel Intentions*	1999	27
Charisma Carpenter	1970	*Buffy the Vampire Slayer*	1997	27
Rebecca Gayheart	1972	*Jawbreaker*	1999	27
Lori Singer	1957	*Footloose*	1984	27
Sissy Spacek	1949	*Carrie*	1976	27
Tobey Maguire	1975	*Spider-Man*	2002	27
Denise Richards	1971	*Wild Things*	1998	27
Kevin Bacon	1958	*Footloose*	1984	26
Jamie Kennedy	1970	*Scream*	1996	26
Matthew Lillard	1970	*Scream*	1996	26
Skeet Ulrich	1970	*Scream*	1996	26
Paul Walker	1973	*She's All That*	1999	26
Scott Wolf	1968	*Party of Five*	1994	26
Minka Kelly	1980	*Friday Night Lights*	2006	26
Ian Ziering	1964	*Beverly Hills, 90210*	1990	26

Before you fire off the "Hey, dummy you forgot...." email, there are hundreds of 23-, 24- and 25-year-old actors who played teens and we certainly can't list them all here. I'm sure there's some creepy website out there devoted to this nonsense. Google it.

Sports News

Ultra-Marathoner Admits He Just Hates His Family

"To be completely honest, I despise running, HATE IT! Competing in these insane 100-mile running races all weekend long and all the training that goes with it is utter torture," said ultra-marathoner Marc Skednick of Philadelphia as he applied super glue to a heel blister the size of a plum. "That said, I continue to do it because I hate spending time with my family a thousand times more than competing in this ridiculous sport."

"My strict training method consists of running about 20 to 30 miles a day in preparation for my weekend races that take place twice a month. As you can see it doesn't allow much time for me to spend with my nagging wife or bratty kids. ... actually, it leaves absolutely no face time for me and my family. I'm really not sure what the 12-year-old looks like now. Or is she 14? Not sure, anyway, gotta motor..." Skednick finishes tending to his wound, slowly gets up and continues his daily run as the clock strikes 10:45 pm.

The 6-foot-1, 135-pound Skednick runs for a few hours before and after work and usually eats all his meals while running. In keeping with his family-shunning ways, Skednick makes sure to take off his Bluetooth before a run just in case a family member might want to get in touch. "I pretend to need 'total concentration' while running, so I ask my family not to call me."

When asked if he misses seeing his daddy, Skednick's 10-year-old son quickly responds, "Do you want to play Guitar Hero? Or go kill some ants?" before he darts into the other room to punch his sister in the back of her head.

His wife Nancy puts her husband's hobby into perspective, "It keeps him happy. He sure seems to love it!"

The long-long-distance runner describes his upcoming 135-mile event, "Like most of the races, this one is in the desert, about a million degrees. I usually puke on average about ten times a day from dehydration and exhaustion but that doesn't deter me, not even the hallucinations can stop me. It's sooooo much better than watching dance recitals and soccer games."

"I'm motivated by that 'Not-seeing-my-family-high' that many runners get after logging in a few miles on the pavement. It makes all the leg cramps, eroded cartilage, third-degree sunburn, pants crapping, and the intense stabbing pain that jets up through my spine every time I begin to move my feet all worth it."

Free Band Names!

- **Nerd Flu** - taken by a emo-alternative band from Nevada.

- **Wait Lifters** - taken by a five-piece rock band from England.

- **16 Pound Baby Girl** - taken by a band from Grundarfjordur, Iceland.

- **Snap Judgment** - taken by a Christian rock band from GA.

- **You're Free to Do as We Say** - taken by a UK indie band.

- **Shippers & Handlers** - taken by a rock band from Ohio.

- **Finland Feels Fine** - taken by a hard rock band from Texas.

- **Borderline Dwellers** – taken by a punk/metal band from VA.

- **Full View Failures** - taken by a two-member punk band from the UK.

- **The Deceivables** - taken by a three-man punk band from NY.

McDonald's Offers New Value "Dime Menu"

Looking to offer something new and exciting to its ever-growing customer base and to get a leg up on the heated competition, McDonald's announced today it is now offering a new "Dime Menu" at all of its restaurants around the country. Everything on this extensive menu will be value priced at ten cents.

"We tried the Dollar Menu thing, and it worked well," said McDonaldland national spokesman Chuck Lartasse. "But what about those who have less than a dollar to spend on food? Huh? That's where this brilliant, new offering comes in. If you have one thin dime, one-tenth of a buck, well partner, we got some truly tasty food for you!"

Here's a sneak peek at some new offerings on the budget-friendly menu:

- **The "Shake Shot"** - Enjoy two ounces of your favorite creamy McDonald's Milkshake (strawberry only) served in a paper shot glass.

- **The One-Piece Chicken McNugget** - Gobble up one hearty piece of crispy chicken (sauce is extra).

- **The Lil' Mac** - Enjoy this fun-sized sandwich jam-packed with pickles, ketchup, salt and pepper served on a seedless bun (sesame seeds and meat extra).

- **Three French Fries** - Have one golden delicious fry now, save two for later or share with friends!

- **Hot Fudge Sundae Cherry** - Why waste your time with the whole sundae when the delectable cherry is the only thing you really want! Mmmm... McFruity!

- **Nothin' McMuffin** - This is the perfect morning meal for those who want a quick, easy breakfast. Savor the top half of a tasty bite-sized English muffin (nooks included, crannies extra).

- **Lite Salad** - Extra-large lettuce leaf sprinkled with water and a single soy crouton. Served with a side of air.

- **Fancy Ketchup Combo** - Slather on the good stuff! Get two (that's right two!) packets of this delish popular tomato-based condiment.

- **The McBite** - For just a dime, our valued customers can take one large bite of any regular sandwich on our entire menu. Chomp away (once) and enjoy the mouth-watering goodness of a Big Mac, a Quarter Pounder or any hot and yummy sandwich you please! (Please note, overly large-sized mouths will be charged extra).

- **Filet-O-Goldfish** - Marinated in water... so moist!

- **Honey Mustard Snack Wrap** - No chicken, just everyone's favorite condiment slathered on a wrap.

- **Bacon, Egg & Cheese McLittle McGriddle** - It takes longer to say than eat! Better grab three!

- **Sixteenth Pounder without Cheese** - Our answer to the poular "Slider," only a fourth of the size for easier *sliding*!

Multicultural Guest Service Enhances Suburban Parties

Gerry and Maddie McMonahan of Paoli, PA, wanted to impress their new neighbors in their development with their "hip" friends from their old neighborhood, but sadly, they had none. That is, until they saw an ad for Party People in The House, LLC, in Philadelphia magazine.

Known as Party Peeps, the year-old Philadelphia-based company offers a rainbow of ethnic and cultural "city types" who will gladly attend the most mundane suburban shindigs and pretend to be the client's best friends, college roommates, ex-lovers, or former traveling companions, showing all in attendance just how cultured and connected the host is.

"We always wanted some black friends but didn't know where to find them or what to say to them when we did," said Gerry as he was preparing for his gathering by hiding his Sports Illustrated, Entertainment Weekly and People magazines and strategically replacing them on the Ikea coffee table with the latest issues of Art Forum, The Economist and Vibe. "Party Peeps made it nice and easy for us because they offer a wide selection of types," Gerry added with a giggle. "I don't know where they find these people!"

The company makes it easy for the most buttoned-down Caucasian professionals to spice up their soirées with interesting multicultural people who will pep things up with their outré dress, worldly accents and the much-needed ability to start impromptu dance parties.

Diverse Roster

Party Peeps offers a large menu of colorful "characters" guaranteed to add some flavor (and flava!) to any fête, captivating guests with their choice of diverse lifestyles, fascinating professions and abstruse interests. Invite one, or chose a group of these "party peeps" a la carte. Here's a sampling of the menu:

Acerbic, Intellectual/Stylish Gay - The real ones are hard to find without this service. "You know, give me one like the guys on Project Runway!" customers proclaim

Hispanic Deejay - Edgy; extra charge for turntables and records

Serious Black Artist/Intellectual - Wearing traditional African garb and wire-rim spectacles (gray dreads optional)

Sexy Grad Student from Italy or Greece - Both genders available! Always ready to flirt Mediterranean-style with your guests

The Well-Heeled Wine Expert - Older, genteel gent in corduroy blazer ready to expound on the virtues of whatever fine "vintages" you were able to scrounge from the clearance bin at Discount Liquor Barn

Important Japanese Filmmaker - Chain-smokes and constantly talks about his (or her!) love of Jimi Hendrix and Yasmine Bleeth

Cute Asian-Girl Designer - Who is obsessed with Hello Kitty and all things Sanrio

Prim-but-Sexy British Couple - Equipped with posh accents and wonderfully saucy stories; think Hugh Grant and Emma Thompson

Alterna-Chick - Caustic, dismissive (claims to have no idea what Desperate Housewives is) yet oddly approachable

Saucy Woman of a Certain Age - One part Mrs. Roper, one part Mrs. Robinson, she's frowsy, blowsy, and doesn't act her age!

Singer-Songwriter Guy - Scruffily handsome and a good listener, possibly kickin' the habit (extra charge for acoustic guitar)

Australian World Traveler - Will put up with every lame Crocodile Dundee reference your guests make and show off his alligator-wrestling scars with very little prompting

Mysterious Psychic/Spiritualist - Enchants all with spot-on predictions and ornate dress and accessories (also very slutty); think of a young Stevie Nicks. Also available: Drag Psychic

Activists - Will tell you what's wrong with everything

Computer Guy in Band - He's got big hands and feet and still wears black jeans; he will tell you how to install proper virus protection or how lame the latest Modest Mouse CD is.

"We also ordered two authentic Irish guys, um, I mean blokes!" beamed Maddie as she unwrapped recently purchased Ludacris and Clancy Brothers CDs recommended through Party Peeps's optional music consulting service. "They're going to pretend to be my cousins from County Clare. Being Irish is very in. Ron [owner of Party Peeps] said not worry if they drop the 'C' or 'F' words a lot because they do it in a charming, inoffensive way. I'm so looking forward to this!"

Ready to Impress

All "party people" are given a one-page fact sheet about the host(s) before the festivities so they are fully prepared to profess their fondness for their "old friend" and bring up a flattering tale at a moment's notice. Dramatizations (actual dialogue may vary):

The Singer-Songwriter: "Jake and I go way back! We were in this ska-punk band back in high school. He was crazy, a rebel, but very smart too! It was tough turning down that major-label deal, but knowing Jake could finish up his accounting degree at Purdue made it worthwhile."

Alterna-Chick: "Christy and I traveled Europe for, like, an entire year and hit every museum from the Uffizi to the Hermitage. In St. Petersburg, we were almost kidnapped by Russian mobsters. She's trouble, let me tell ya!"

Party characters are priced at a reasonable hourly rate, and there is a discount when you rent five professional guests or more. To keep in character, all pro guests will show up fashionably late and make a grand entrance. "Sorry, we were just at What-His-Face's latest show at the So-and-So Gallery!"

Party Peeps is also perfect for the single person looking to dazzle new dates. "I just started seeing this chick who reads books and knows a lot about art and crap," said restaurant supplier Justin Ivoryson. "She wanted to meet my friends, and I realized my crew just plays Playstation all day and goes to sports bars. Then I heard about Party Peeps and asked them to send over some smart folks pronto. It worked like a charm! Two drama queens and one German art professor later, and I'm so in!"

The hosts are not the only ones enjoying this fantastic new party staffing service. The freelance party peeps, many of whom are pursuing careers as actors, really enjoy the work.

"It's a bit excruciating the first hour or so, lots of whispering, pointing and some hiding of valuables," said actor, dancer, deejay and hired party guest Marco Mendes. "But once the drinks kick in, everyone is eager to chat me up and ask about my tattoos, my tan and my equipment."

- Additional reporting by Scott Shrake.

Free Band Names!

- **Bad in Tents** - taken by a punk metal band from Alaska.

- **Fixins' Bar** - taken by a four-piece punk/rock band from Australia.

- **AdoraBully** - taken by two folky/alternative acoustic girls from WA.

- **We've Got Clout, Yes We Do** - taken by a two-piece rock band from AK.

- **The Threepenny Bits** - taken by a hard rock/metal band from WA.

- **Natural Male Enhancement** - taken by a emo punk band from MO.

- **Depth Hoar** - taken by a New Wave band from England.

Hollywood Height Chart

For no reason at all, here is a list of heights of your favorite and not-so-favorite celebrities. Heights were taken from IMDB.com. Some are accurate but most are blatant lies put forth by the celeb's publicists for vanity's sake. We all know Denzel is nowhere near 6 foot and our boy Frodo is 5'6" only if he stands on Peter Jackson's giant lunch bag. See where you stack up!

HEIGHT	CELEBRITY	FAMOUS FOR...
2' 8"	Verne Troyer	Mini Me; Dating models
3' 4"	Emmanuel Lewis	Hugging George Papadapolis
4' 3"	Zelda Rubinstein	"This house is clean!"
4' 6"	Jason Acuña	Wee Man from "Jackass"
4' 8"	Gary Coleman	Onetime gubernatorial candidate
4' 9"	Linda Hunt	The Year of Living Dangerously
4' 11"	Lil' Kim	Giant unwieldy breasts
5' 0"	Danny DeVito	Marrying equally ugly human
5' 1"	Janeane Garofalo	Angering conservatives
5' 1"	Kristin Bell	America's favorite teen detective
5' 2"	Paul Williams	70s songwriter with Cousin It hair
5' 2"	Paula Abdul	Giving useless feedback
5' 2½"	Dudley Moore	Climbing Susan Anton
5' 2½"	Julia Louis-Dreyfus	No one "Watching Ellie"
5' 3"	Prince	Being overrated (sorry everyone!)
5' 3"	Ashley Olsen	Eating more than her sister
5' 4"	Rachel Bilson	Summer on "The O.C."
5' 4"	Seth Green	Scott Evil from Austin Powers
5' 4½"	Raven Symoné	Getting decent work after "Cosby"

HEIGHT	CELEBRITY	FAMOUS FOR...
5' 5"	Michael J. Fox	Hanging with Skippy Handleman
5' 5"	Jennifer Aniston	Hair; nipples
5' 6"	Elijah Wood	Fighting off Samwise's advances
5' 6"	Penélope Cruz	Dating Tom Cruise
5' 6½"	Henry Winkler	Having urinals in his office
5' 6½"	Farrah Fawcett	Feathered hair; Doing a bionic guy
5' 7"	Oprah Winfrey	Supporting Steadman; Weight gains
5' 7"	Tom Cruise	Denying gay rumors
5' 7½"	Sandra Bullock	Not passing on *Speed 2*
5' 8"	Ben Stiller	Working at P.J. O' Pootertoot's
5' 8"	Angelina Jolie	Adopting children
5' 8½"	Don Cheadle	*Oceans Eleven*; *Hotel Rawanda*
5' 8½"	Catherine Zeta-Jones	Marrying old
5' 8½"	Mark Wahlberg	Wearing underwear
5' 9"	Paul Newman	*Cool Hand Luke*; salad dressing
5' 9"	Joan Cusack	Awesome headgear in *16 Candles*
5' 9½"	Matt Damon	Wisely distancing himself from Ben
5' 9½"	Heidi Klum	Having her photo taken
5' 10"	Colin Farrell	Keeping Irish stereotypes alive
5' 10"	Katie Holmes	Choosing Pacey, Marrying famous
5' 10"	Michael Cera	Playing himself
5' 10½"	Nicole Kidman	Looking bothered and superior
5' 11"	George Clooney	Killing *Batman* franchise
5' 11"	Gisele Bundchen	Dating Leo
5' 11½"	Brad Pitt	Dumping Gwyneth and Jennifer
6' 0"	Denzel Washington	*Carbon Copy*; *Philadelphia*
6' 0"	Geena Davis	Thelma & Louise; Archery
6' 0"	Brooke Shields	Taking on Tom Cruise

HEIGHT	CELEBRITY	FAMOUS FOR...
6' 1"	Vin Diesel	XXX; being bald
6' 1"	Keanu Reeves	Saying "Whoa..."
6' 2"	Jim Carrey	Fire Marshall Bill Burns
6' 2½"	John Cusack	"Ohhhh. Tentacles. N-T."
6' 2½"	Bernie Mac	Eponymous sitcom
6' 3"	Paul Walker	Being fast and furious
6' 3"	Gabrielle Reece	Volleyball; *Air Bud: Spikes Back*
6' 3"	John Krasinski	Big tuna
6' 3½"	Will Ferrell	Frank the Tank; playing cowbell
6' 4"	Ruben Studdard	Not eating Clay
6' 4"	Dwayne Johnson	Raising his eyebrow
6' 4½"	Conan O'Brien	Fantastic hair
6' 5"	Vince Vaughn	"You're so fucking money, baby..."
6' 5"	Lisa Leslie	Sexy WNBA superstar
6' 6"	Mark Curry	TV's Mr. Cooper
6' 7"	James Arness	Matt Dillon from "Gunsmoke"
6' 8"	Richard Moll	Bull on "Night Court"
6' 8½"	Brad Garrett	Loving Raymond
6' 9"	Ted Cassidy	Lurch on the "Addam's Family"
7' 1"	Shaquille O'Neal	Kazaam; Fu-Schnickens
7' 1½"	André The Giant	"Anybody want a peanut?"
7' 2"	Richard Kiel	"Jaws" from James Bond movies
7' 3"	Peter Mayhew	"Chewbacca" from *Star Wars*
7' 3"	Sandy Allen	World's Tallest Woman
7' 7"	Gheorghe Muresan	Stinking at basketball; *My Giant*
7' 9"	Radhouane Charbib	World's Tallest Living Man

Entertainment News

Dismissed Reality Show Contestant Vows to Disappear

In what appears to be a reality show first, that contestant you really didn't care one way or the other about who just got eliminated from that reality show you kinda like, ended her brief and unspectacular stint on the show by saying,

"Hey America, this is definitely the last you will see of me!"

"Yep, I'm done."

She continued speaking to the camera with absolutely no emotion.

"This wasn't a great learning experience for me, I did not listen to one word the judges said and I most definitely did not become great friends with any of the other contestants."

After wiping away no tears, she added, "I am taking nothing away from this and I will no doubt go back home to no loved ones and absolutely not continue in this profession. I hope you didn't get too attached because I really have nothing left to offer. That was it, America. So don't look for updates on my Facebook or MySpace pages because they don't exist."

As the camera rolls and she packed her bags and tools of the trade, she added, "I almost forgot, I wanted to thank no one."

She finished her post-show interview saying how she looks forward to not cashing in on her brief fame by never appearing at local bars and hosting body shot and wet T-shirt competitions.

Photoshop Now Offers "Family Beach Photo" Generator

If you belong to a loving, handsome family who cherish time spent together, chances are you have an impressive golden-hued photo over your mantle showing your smiling, sun-kissed clan huddled together in matching outfits at the beach.

For many, such an extravagance is only a dream due to the time and logistics of gathering everyone together for a laborious, expensive professional shoot that will most likely end in a family squabble.

Adobe Photoshop, the industry standard for digital photography, hopes to change that. It now offers a "Family Beach Photo" generator that will quickly and easily create a gorgeous, large format photo of your family on a virtual beach with just a couple quick clicks of the mouse. Now travel-adverse Midwesterners and heliophobes alike, who've never stepped foot on a sandy shore, can take part in this timeless American tradition.

34

Open the application and a user-friendly step-by-step generator will guide you through the composition of your portrait. It will first prompt you to open a photo of your family (digital or scanned in, whatever you have handy) and select just the heads of your family members, one at a time, with the easy-to-use selection tool. Save the heads and designate their roles ("Dad," "Oldest Sister," "Baby" etc.).

Add as many members a you like. Want dearly departed Grandpa in the shot? No problem, just add his head and he's getting his barefoot toes just as sandy as the rest of the living brood. Trying hard to forget drug-addled middle brother and his lengthy prison record? Again, no problem, just leave him out and your family's purity is preserved.

Once you've finished adding heads, the real he fun begins as you start customizing your keepsake. Here's a glance at some of the options available.

Beach Location

Choose sunrise or sunset at the following picturesque, sandy beaches:

- Nantucket, MA
- Spring Lake, NJ
- Easthampton, NY
- Malibu, CA

Focal Point

Choose one of these beachy favorites for your family to sit upon and surround:

- Dunes
- Jetty
- Lifeguard stand
- Rustic rowboat

Time of Day

- Sunrise
- Sunset
- Chilly autumn afternoon

Attire

Your entire family will be dressed in matching outfits for maximum cuteness and togetherness. Options include:

- Shirts: white tees, white oxfords or white golf shirts
- Pants: khakis, jeans or khaki shorts

Body Type

Haven't had time to diet or workout before the shoot? No worry, there are hundreds of body types to choose from. Look realistic or go for the idealized you. Here's a sampling available for Dad:

- Pudgy golfer
- Slouchy CPA
- Rail-thin marathoner
- Buff lumberjack

Pose and Layout

Choose position and posture of each family member. If Dad and Sis haven't spoken in years, a warm photo embrace between the two might rekindle better days and heal the rift.

- Sitting with crossed legs and clasped hands
- Lying "funny-guy" style across the front row
- Standing with hands thoughtfully placed on sibling's shoulder
- Standing aloof (perfect for moody teen)
- Family pyramid

Tan Level

Don't want that pasty family member ruining the shot with his/her unsightly pallor? Add some summertime color in a flash! The generator offers numerous sunny skin tones (making sure to match face with body). Here are a few presets:

- Crisp Irish crimson
- Weathered fisherman

- ◆ Mochaccino
- ◆ Guido brown
- ◆ Slutty bronze

Teeth Whitener

The only yellow you'll see is in the lush rays or the gentle sunlight thanks to the "Pearly Whites" filter. Choose your level of teeth whitening:

- ◆ White
- ◆ Bright white
- ◆ Blue white
- ◆ Chiclets
- ◆ Radioactive Regis Philbin white

Additional Elements

Add some subtle touches to the photo to give it some extra warmth, class and character:

- ◆ Family dog (golden retriever only)
- ◆ Seagull (clean and white, not the filthy NJ type)
- ◆ Football (for Kennedy-style pickup games)
- ◆ Soft breeze (gently blowing hair)
- ◆ Wicker picnic basket

Bonus Engagement Photo Filter!

Get a romantic remembrance of your current (or past) relationship, suitable for local newspaper engagement announcements. All gender combinations available. Take your pick of scenarios:

- ◆ Classic hand-on-shoulder ring pose
- ◆ Seated snuggle
- ◆ Playful clinch
- ◆ Passionate make-out

Smokers Stay Healthy in The Workplace

According to the latest Occupational Safety & Health Administration (OSHA) report, people who smoke cigarettes are significantly less likely to fall victim to workplace injuries.

OSHA spokesperson Jerry Reinert explains, "Because your average smoker spends a third of his/her day outside of the office smoking cigarettes, they are at least 33% less likely to acquire Carpal Tunnel Syndrome, Repetitive Stress Disorder, severe eyestrain and other workplace hazards that befall your average diligent worker."

"Simply put, the more you are away from your desk not performing work, the healthier you are."

This is wonderful news to those workers who enjoy and depend on the sweet, mellow flavor of nicotine and menthol to help them through the daily grind. Sad to say, smokers are seen as pariahs in today's health-conscious society and find it very difficult to enjoy their favorite pastime during the work day without receiving nasty looks and comments from the smoke-free world.

"Yeah, some people sneer at me when I smoke. They think I'm gross or don't care about my health. That's bull. Except for the smoking thing, I'm a pretty healthy person. With all the time I spend outside during the work day, I would even consider myself outdoorsy," explains Marie Tocheretto, a marketing coordinator for Xerchtech Inc., in between drags of her third cigarette of the morning. "I love being outdoors. Smoking gives me this opportunity, and I am thankful for that."

Mike Brown, a programmer and fellow puffer, adds, "I used to get severe eyestrain and headaches from staring at the computer all day. I didn't know what to do. Then after watching Marie, I realized if I just smoked I could leave my desk whenever I wanted and go outside for a nice 20-minute break. So now I've taken up smoking (two packs a day)! I duck outside every now and then (about six to seven breaks a day) and my eyestrain and headaches have virtually disappeared. It's great!"

Many people are stuck in their cubes all day — working, emailing, eating, napping — and have little chance for quality interpersonal contact. Not so for smokers. Go to any office park by the back door, alley, stairwell or bathroom and you'll see a gregarious group of people from different backgrounds talking, laughing, catching up, and of course, relaxing with a cig.

Studies* show smokers have an easier time meeting ("Hey, you got a light?") and talking ("Can I bum a cigarette?") to people they don't know.

"I met my wife on a smoke break!" added Mike.

Smoking is also therapeutic. "Cindy has a lot of problems at home right now with Roger and his drinking. She usually needs to talk with me three of four times a day. I'm a good friend and a good listener, so I don't mind the inconvenience," relates personal assistant Angie Hackforth. "We could never talk openly in the office. Too many nosy nellies getting in other people's business. Smoke breaks allow us private time to talk... time to heal."

A severe smoking habit may bring on a little cough and damage the lungs, but these organs are hidden inside the body (the average person hardly notices them). Keeping the limbs, eyes and other external body parts healthy is a much bigger concern.

So if you want to keep the important parts of your body in tip-top shape (and make some friends in the process), go outside, get some air and spark one up!

*1999 American Tobacco Association report "Smoke Your Way to Friendship."

Listless Effort

Your St. Patrick's Day To-Do List

It's *always* time to honor everyone's favorite excuse to join a pub crawl. Slainte!

1. Take off slightly-stained B.U.M Equipment sweatshirt, put on very-stained Notre Dame sweatshirt.

2. Start off the special day right with McMuffin and Shamrock Shake.

3. Fill empty shake cup with whiskey and march in parade.

4. Leave parade after 10 minutes. Enter favorite Irish bar.

5. Call "Sully" and "Murph" to let them know just how wasted you already are.

6. Clap at the wrong times while singing along with "The Wild Rover."

7. Aggressively tongue kiss fat drunk girl in between bites of corned beef sandwich.

8. Do "Cabbage Patch" dance over and over until somebody gets the Irish reference.

9. Keep your shtick going and bust out your funny "Riverdance" routine.

10. Due to exhaustion, pass out in alley behind bar, reappear in bar one hour later completely invigorated.

11. Strategically place "Kiss Me I'm Irish" pin on fly. Harass every female within 20-foot radius.

12. Instigate a donnybrook.

13. Nod your head as friends discuss Shane MacGowan and act like you know who the hell he is.

14. Acquire brogue. Pretend you're from Ireland. Fool no one.

15. Not bat an eye at the plastered woman holding a 4-month-old in the smoky, crowded bar.

16. Hunt down actual Irish person; proceed to bore him to tears with your strikingly limited knowledge of the Emerald Isle, including the mispronounced names of the counties where your great great grandparents might have lived.

17. Spout anti-English sentiments and proclaim your admiration for the boys in "The I.R.S." (you mean I.R.A.).

18. Act like bagpipes aren't the worst sound you've ever heard.

19. Spill entire pint of Guinness on stranger. Get in fistfight with stranger. Hug stranger. Introduce stranger to everyone as your new best friend.

20. Wake up in puddle of puke (not your own) and realize its only 3:00 pm. Leave men's room and continue drinking.

Technology News

Blog Gives Detailed Account of New Laundry Basket Purchase

If you're like most people with a healthy sense of curiosity, you often find yourself whiling away the hours thinking about what type of laundry basket a successful creative director at a big-time New York ad agency uses and the reasons behind the purchase.  Before the dawn of the information-rich Internet, quenching this thirst would be near impossible.

Now thanks to Micah Josten and his daily blog (*No Sleep in Brooklyn Bee-atches*), the average joe can now enjoy a no-holds-barred, insider view of not only what type of laundry basket Josten currently uses, but also a blow-by-blow account of the how, what, when, where and why he decided to purchase the white Rubbermaid Hip Hugger© Laundry Basket and why the other baskets didn't measure up.

Jansen puts in solid 10-plus hour days at his agency, but still finds time to update his blog and let the world now how he "kicks it" in his Brooklyn neighborhood, detailing every facet of his life – from his love of the new Scissor Sisters CD, PBR cans and vintage tees to his fear of his "old-school" corner bar becoming too "trendy." While these frequent missives are fascinating in their own right and viewed by "more people than you'd ever believe... my page views are insane," they pale in comparison to the finely detailed treatment he gives to his acquisitions, both large and small.

Most recently, he sent shockwaves through the blogging community with a prolix post extolling his functional yet stylish white laundry basket, replete with an ergonomic, curved design, three sturdy grab-through handles and the heavy-duty construction and smooth finish that one comes to expect from a quality Rubbermaid product. Josten feels an immense sense of pride that his review will help educate all those contemplating buying a new basket. One reader comment posted 39 minutes after the initial post read:

> "Cool. I'll check it out if mine ever wears out... BTW, can I borrow your 'Alias: Season Three' DVD? - Sam"

Many bloggers would be content giving their faithful readers a passing mention that they picked up a new laundry basket at the local Bed Bath and Beyond after grabbing coffee and picking up some fresh clementines at their favorite Korean grocer, but that is where the normal "amateur" blogger and Josten differ. Josten describes his 1,300-word entry dedicated to the purchase of his basket as "Just the way I do things, bro. I give it 100% or don't do it at all."

Sample text from Blog entry entitled "A Tisket a Tasket, A Brand New Laundry Basket":

> "After test driving some twenty-odd other baskets (don't worry, I didn't actually sit in them and steer them around the aisles! LOL) in the five stores I've visited today, I have narrowed my decision down to two models. While I love the aesthetics of the Home Willow Laundry Basket with its rustic charm, I am a bit concerned the wicker will wear down in time and the edges might poke through, posing a threat to my clothes. Rubbermaid Hip Hugger Laundry Basket with its smooth finish will surely prevent any snagging of my delicate items. To really seal the deal, I went looking for a store associate to check on any warranty info he or she might have on the products."

Despite the time and dedication it takes to write such exhaustive entries on his blog — six posts per day on average — do not be fooled. Josten is extremely busy and in no way does this activity get in the way of his day job or interfere with his social life.

"I'm just an expert at multi-tasking and optimizing my time," Josten said as he types in a new entry, speaks on his cell and stirs his steaming cup of herbal tea at his desk. "That's why the hip-hugging feature of my new laundry basket was so crucial in my decision-making process. This simple yet ingenious functionality allows me to hold a full basket of clothes with only one hand and my hip, freeing up my other hand to Twitter about how the stain removal went."

Listless Effort

Best American Bands Ever? A Haiku Review

A while back, a writer for some newspaper was hurting for a column so she resorted to using an old favorite, "The Reader's Poll." An informal survey was taken asking readers to name "The Greatest American Rock Band of All Time." I decided to respond and critique the readers' choices using a very concise and effective method, the Haiku. In case you were sleeping through 5th grade English class (I was), a Haiku is a 17-syllable verse form consisting of three metrical units of 5, 7, and 5 syllables.

01. **Pearl Jam**
Outstanding live act,
but bad actors (See "Singles").
I don't miss flannel.

02. **Aerosmith**
They ruled when on coke.
Sobered up and lost all cred.
Crap songs for crap films.

03. **Van Halen**
Hagar's a buffoon.
He is Jimmy Buffet Lite.
Roth? Better buffoon.

04. **The Eagles**
They hate each other
but regrouped for love of fans
and assloads of cash.

05. **Journey**
Schon's afro was huge
when he played with Santana.
Perry had girl hair.

06. **Guns N' Roses**
The best band ever
for those who have shit for brains.
Viva la dirtbags!

07. **The Grateful Dead**
Garcia is gone
but smelly, lazy hippies
will live forever.

08. **Queensryche**
This poll was taken
during a county fair where
Queensryche was playing.

09. **The Doors**
Did you see the film?
Man, Kilmer looked just like him!
"Real Genius," better.

10. **R.E.M.**
"Murmur" was amazing.
"Life's Rich Pageant" also ruled.
What was Stipe saying?

11. **The Allman Brothers Band and Fleetwood Mac (tie)**
A fight to the death
with broad swords and hunting
knives
will break this tie!

12. **Metallica**
Keeps on putting out
dumb music for dumb people.
Philly Radio!

13. **Kiss**
Calling all Kiss fans!
Want to buy a Kiss coffin?
Gene Simmons: a total dick.

14. **The Ramones**
T-shirts all around!
Jonas Brother now wears one.
Good time to burn yours.

15. **Bruce Springsteen & The E Street Band and Creedence Clearwater Revival (tie)**
I lived on Tenth Ave.,
the same street Bruce sang about.
Never saw a "freeze out."

16. **Dave Matthews Band and Lynyrd Skynyrd (tie)**
Lame, drunk guy at show
always yells, "Play some
Skynyrd!"
No one ever laughs.

17. **The Beach Boys**
TV's John Stamos
plays drums for the Boys sometimes.
Those times really blow.

18. **Nirvana**
One awesome album
then a couple decent ones.
A good band, not great.

19. **The Replacements**
Made rockin' music
while they were very hammered.
Three cheers for liquor!

20. **Bon Jovi**
All over Jersey
their aging, cheeseball fans ask,
"Where are John's eyebrows?"

Man Prefers Kiddie Pool Over Beach

As summer approaches, the denizens of the small NJ beach town of Belmar can look forward to the sights, sounds and smells of the season — hotdogs grilling on the barbeque, sunscreen #30 sticking to alabaster bodies and of course, loud drunks holding court in kiddie pools.

One drunk in particular, Louie Iadochico, a 27-year-old stockbroker trainee from Staten Island, spends the majority of his summer weekends sitting happily in his inflatable, 5-foot diameter kiddie pool.

This plastic oasis is positioned front and center on the lawn of the 10th avenue rental house he shares with thirteen other buddies. The three-bedroom house is only one block away from the beach, but the proximity is still not a big enough draw to make Louie leave the safe confines of his aquatic throne.

Pool Rules

"The pool effin rules!" Declares a visibly inebriated Louie sitting spread eagle in his pool. "Why drag my sexy ass down to the beach when I got everything I need right here. Can you drink beer on the beach? No. Can you smoke cigarettes on the beach? Not this year. Can you pee on the beach without getting up? No. Well I can do it all right here."

Another favorite pastime of Louie and pals is making time with the ladies.

"By sitting in the pool all day, I get to see all the talent walk by on their way to the beach. When a hottie walks by I usually wink and say, 'It's all good!' or 'There's room in here for two, baby.' and I'll offer them a beer. If some skanky ho walks by, I'll just tell her, 'Keep walking, ain't nothing to see here.' or something funny like that. It really cracks the guys up."

Louie fills up his pool with fresh water every Friday afternoon when he arrives. By Saturday afternoon there is usually about eight beer cans and some soggy hamburger rolls accompanying him in the pool. There are also about 20 to 30 small stones.

"Louie usually passes out around three or four o'clock for a solid two hours," relates amused housemate Anthony Mastrorilli. "That when me, Sal and Reilly put a bottle on Louie's head and try to knock it off with these little rocks," he says as he picks up a handful of stones from the driveway. "That fat bastard never wakes up. He's out cold. It's the only time he shuts the eff up."

Annoyed Neighbors

Some of the neighbors are year-round residents and do not appreciate the unsavory sight of a large, hairy man basting in a kiddie pool and spewing profane language.

"Most of them are decent kids. They just play wiffleball for a good six to eight hours a day or put a TV on the lawn and watch the Mets game," says Fred Tozzi, a Belmar resident who lives across the street from the rental property.

"A couple of them though have real potty mouths, especially the big fella in the pool. He never gets up. I think he's disabled."

David Blaine Fails Latest Stunt

In what was billed as the brazen magician's most courageous and impossible stunt to date, David Blaine officially gave up his quest to work as an assistant product manager at a technology company for one straight month (with weekends off). After a mere 16 hours in the harrowing position, Blaine took a long lunch and never returned.

"I met my match," said a gaunt and sickly looking Blaine, who had survived the treacherous two-day period by subsisting on only 12 cups of tepid company coffee and various sugared snacks and pretzels from the vending machines. "Physically, I was in good shape at the start. But the pervasive soul-sucking environment of the office and the overwhelming sense of anomie that the workers exuded completely sapped me of my will to perform... my will to live."

The much-heralded daredevil who has survived such stunts as being buried alive and being turned into a human ice cube, has never had a real day job and did not know what to expect. After his first 10-hour day, filled with four different meetings and two conference calls with needy clients, Blaine was extremely fatigued and found wandering around the kitchen in a daze looking for coffee creamers.

"The meetings were killers and so damn long, and we didn't even touch on all the points we needed to. But my workspace was the real nail in the coffin," continued Blaine as he was been given liquids intravenously.

"The cube was so just insanely small, even for me, an experienced contortionist, that I could not physically do my work. Plus I was distracted by my coworker who was on the phone with her husband every 10 minutes and my manager Todd who kept Instant Messaging me about my progress."

Blaine was also stymied by the work that was given to him. "I just could not get the goddamn graphics to import correctly into the PowerPoint presentation that I was supposed to have ready for my 2:00pm meeting with Marketing. It was freaking impossible. My magic was powerless."

Blaine said he is not sure of his next stunt and might just take some time off and relax with twin Brazilian supermodels in the Hamptons.

New Baby Names Found in Your Home

With our schools being overrun with Madisons, Emmas, Connors and Jacks, we must find new inspiration when naming our children. Look no further than the safe confines of your home. Just open the cabinets!

- Smucker
- Pam
- Beano
- Oral B.
- Cremora
- Flonase
- Ortega
- Comet
- Summer Eve
- Stouffer

- Drano
- Brawny
- Baco
- Dixie
- Monistat 7
- Swanson
- Charmin
- Borden
- Eukanuba
- Sparkle

Nudity Trounces Modesty in Men's Locker Room

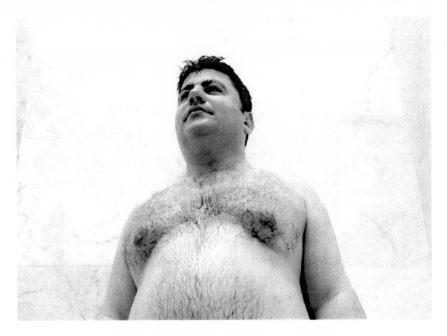

If you're an aficionado of the nude male form and all its absurdly wondrous variations, there is no better place for your viewing enjoyment than the YMCA Men's locker room in Athensville, PA, where bare-ass nakedness reigns supreme. Putting on clothes after a refreshing shower is not a speedy and rushed-through process for the majority of these gregarious gym guys of all ages who swim, work out and socialize at the Y.

In fact, these slow dressers prefer to march about the industrial carpeted floors au naturel, allowing their various flapping folds of flesh to swing freely and hang about as they chat to one another about sports, work and other sundry conversations. Distended, rotund paunches and hirsute, hunched backs dripping with sweat mingle with finely tuned, athletic torsos and ripped delts in grand convivial fashion.

Shy, modest and no-nonsense types once ruled the deodorant-tinged environs, quickly taking off and putting on their gym clothes in glaringly rude silence. Nary a word was uttered between these antisocial, apparel-loving men as they donned their clothes as if they were in some strange clothes-putting-on contest. But times have changed. Men who are comfortable with their bodies — and more importantly, comfortable staring at another fellow's man-breasts or pendulous scrotum as they talk about mortgage rates — now have the freedom to high five, back slap and trade good-natured quips without being weighed down by the oppressive confines of clothing.

Now it's perfectly acceptable to walk straight out of the shower to your locker, stop and chat to a couple of friends for a spell, walk over to the sink area to shave and then proceed to the bathroom stalls for a leisurely number-two without once thinking of grabbing a towel to cover up.

"After a good workout you need to air out your bits and pieces for a while before you put on your clothes," said Thomas Sciarapini, a large bear of a man who just completed an entire issue of Us Weekly as he slowly jogged on a treadmill for his usual 25-minute workout. "If you put your clothes on too soon after your shower and you're still wet, mold or something can build up in those hard to reach places and you don't want that. Yuck!"

Sciarapini continued as he arose from sitting on one of the numerous old wooden benches that have seen and felt their fair share of bare, moist buttocks. "It's better to just walk around and let nature handle the drying process. 20 to 30 minutes should do the trick."

By the looks of the unabashed nudity pervading the locker room during any a normal weeknight, many agree with Sciarapini's corporeal-based scientific reasoning. Still, there are a few members of the old guard who won't give in.

"I just like to get in and get out without much, if any, conversation," said long-time Y member Charles Ryan. "But it's really difficult getting dressed without some nude guy standing in front of you yapping up a storm, talking about the Eagles or worse, asking you if a mole on his thigh might be skin cancer. It always feels like a bad scene from *Oz* might break out at any moment."

Blackwater Unit Joins Army Football Team

In a move to shore up protection for the Black Knights ailing backfield, the coaching staff at the esteemed West Point Military Academy took a page from outgoing President Bush's playbook and contracted Blackwater USA mercenaries to play offensive line.

"Our quarterbacks have been getting beaten up pretty bad lately and we were down to our third-stringer. So we decided to shake things up! We redeployed our current O-line — they're now working in the mess hall — and replaced them with these Blackwater boys. These fellas are really great! Very coachable, disciplined and have that killer instinct we love," said the Army head coach.

"It was hard at first to convince them that a karate chop to the throat and a roundhouse kick to the back of the neck of an opposing player are considered penalties, but we worked out the kinks."

Luckily for West Point, the new offensive linemen have full college eligibility and do not violate any NCAA student athlete regulations because they are not getting paid. Blackwater USA did not seek compensation for their work. In a related story, Secretary of Defense Robert M. Gates approved another 5-year (no-compete), $1 billion contract for Blackwater services under the wire in the Bush presidency.

While the unit's on-field play has been successful, there have been few reports of some small off-field, post-game altercations involving drinking, machine gun fire, kidnapping and throat slitting. "Boys will be boys!" said the coach. "You gotta let off a little steam." Asked how the other players feel about their new teammates, the coach continued.

"They love 'em! Here at the academy we teach real-world situations and our boys appreciate that. In today's military, US troops and highly paid soldiers of fortune with absolute no accountability now work hand-in-hand protecting our county. Having this model on the football field feels very natural...very modern, wouldn't you say?"

While most teammates refused to talk, a defensive player who wished to remain nameless said, "Um, has anyone noticed they have Special Forces survival knives concealed in their socks when they take the field? Just thought I'd mention that."

Health News

Follicopagus Twins Separated!

Doctors in Plano, TX, just completed the first successful separation of follicopagus conjoined twins after a grueling 26-second operation. The 2-year-old twins, Summer and Brittany Muderick, have been joined at the hair since birth and are expected to make a full recovery.

"We went in with a very sharp pair of barber shears, the stainless steel Hirose 7-inch model, and snipped the conjoined ponytail. But first we needed to perform the delicate procedure of removing the pink Hello Kitty bow from the braided tuft of hair that connected the two little girls," said a beaming Dr. David Stella, chief surgeon and leader of the eight-person, "de-conjoining" surgical team.

Most conjoined births occur only once in every 200,000 live births, with the most common type being the thoracopagus variety, where there is an anterior union of the upper half of the twins' trunks. Follicopagus is considered the most rare, with only one case reported to date. "We thought we had a case a few years back, but it turned out the hair was just really tangled, nothing a little leave-in conditioner couldn't fix," said Stella.

While this is the first known successful separation of conjoined-by-the-hair twins, there is a pair of 4-year-old female twins in Italy connected by the moustache, but the surgery is deemed too risky to perform.

Man Beats Cancer, Completes First Triathlon Viewing

"Before I got sick I could never imagine doing something like this," said Kevin Favieri as he relaxed on his basement couch eating a large bowl of Cheese Nips. "But now, after being in remission and feeling good again, I have a whole new perspective and a desire to try new things. I want to really live life now!"

Favieri, an avid football and NASCAR fan, completed watching his first televised triathlon only three months after getting a clean bill of health from his doctor.

"I took it slow at first, only watching the swimming part for a few minutes then I'd turn it off and take a nap. I'd then watch another triathlon and try to make it through the bike leg," Favieri said as he adjusted his flannel pajama bottoms and propped another couch cushion behind his head.

"My friends thought I was crazy. I mean, this isn't fun stuff and takes a lot of determination and focus. It was pretty exhausting, plus, knowing that you are only one of a select few doing this makes it even harder. But I persevered and started getting into it and understanding the mentality it takes to finish. I got in the zone and started enjoying it. It must be like one of those 'runner's highs' I've heard about. Really awesome!"

Defying the naysayers made this personal triumph even sweeter for Favieri. "Two years ago, my doctors thought I was a goner, but I beat cancer and proved them wrong. I took that defiance and never-say-die attitude into the basement with me when I started training. A lot of my pals thought there was no way I could watch an entire triathlon without flipping on something else and getting distracted, especially with all The Hills and I Love Money marathons on at the same time. It was tough; I love when those kids stare at each other and eat bugs and stuff."

On a late August Saturday afternoon with temperatures at a cool 74 degrees (air conditioning setting), Favieri completed his viewing in just under three hours and even watched all the commercials. "The commercials were tedious and I almost bailed, but you gotta be a 100% committed, or just don't do it at all." He then cooled down by watching an hour-long Bowflex infomercial.

Now realizing the world has much more to offer than the same sports he watched for hours on end, Smith now changes the channels with an open mind and stops on such exotic fare as Tour de France, indoor lacrosse and women's nine-ball billiards. "You really learn a lot about yourself when you expand your horizons and your TiVo programming choices."

Taking advantage of his new lease on life, Favieri now gets up at 8:45 a.m. every morning — an entire 45 minutes earlier before the cancer diagnosis — to get in some viewing practice before he starts the day.

Asked if he'd attempt another one soon, Favieri replied, "Definitely, I think I'm getting addicted. But I am hoping there is some sort of 'fantasy triathlon league' online, you know, to add some extra interest."

Favieri takes a moment to reflect.

"I just don't want to live my life saying 'I wish I watched this' or 'I wish I watched that,'" the cancer-survivor relates as he wipes a tear from his eyes and opens another can of beer.

"There's a great big world out there for me to experience. On TV."

Tonight on Your Local News!

What's in Your Child's School Lunch?
RADIOACTIVE

- 🕐 99% of Indians Polled Find Gay Cowboy Movie Very Realistic!

- 🕐 Awareness Bracelets Found to Cause Cancer!

- 🕐 Rogue *Second Life* Avatar Creates *Third Life*, Where He Plays a Bald, Overweight Accountant with 3 Kids!

- 🕐 Trader Joe's Employee Goes from 'Very Friendly' to 'Very Irritating' in a Matter of Seconds!

- 🕐 Rabid Sports Fan Hits Rock Bottom, Joins Fantasy Paintball League!

- 🕐 Kevin Costner and a *Really Bad Premise* Team Up Once Again for New Movie!

- 🕐 Rick James' Ghost Assaults Two Women; Smokes Crack!

- 🕐 'Are You Fatter Than a Fifth Grader?' Gets Green Light on FOX!

- 🕐 Ironic T-Shirts Clash at SXSW Festival, Thousands of Feelings Reported Hurt!

- 🕐 NYC Rats Consider Stomach Stapling to Deal with Rising Obesity Problem!

- Thousands of Viewers Reported Sick After 'The View' Goes High Def!

- NBC's Dateline Catches Last Predator, Internet Now Completely Safe!

- Forensic Experts Reveal *Footprints* Were Not God's; You Were in Fact, Walking Alone during Your Most Troublesome Times!

- Jim Belushi Searches Fruitlessly Online for 'According to Jim' *Save Our Show* Campaign!

- Microsoft Employees Brace for Severe Backlash from Their Disappointed Kids Upon Receipt of Zunes Instead of iPods on Christmas Morning!

- Misplaced Script Found in Martin Scorsese's Eyebrows 20 Years Later!

- Hulk Hogan's Daughter Tests Positive for Gamma Radiation!

- Madonna Adopts Child in Africa, Buys Matching Luggage in Paris!

- Paula Deen Caught Eating an Entire Stick of Butter While Filming Cooking Show!

- Traffic Copter Crashes to Earth, Fiery Carnage Causes Eastbound Delays!

- After Years of Living a Lie, Lead Singer of Toto Admits He's Never Really Been to Africa!

- Despite Numerous Requests, Il Divo Still Refuses to Sing "Whip It" in Concert!

- Child Lost When Mother Over-Mulches Garden Bed, Massive Search Continues!

- Suge Knight 'Punk'd' Episode Goes Horribly Wrong; Cast and Crew Found Dead!

- World Record Set at Spring Training Baseball Game for 'Longest Group Yawn!'

Business News

Much-Heralded Office Shower Becomes Less-Heralded Storage Area

After 26 months of almost 100-percent inactivity, OviTech Solutions' office shower has been designated the new official storage area for copy paper, file folders and presentation binders. Office manager Pam Superstein made the announcement in an intra-office email.

The audibly disappointed Superstein described the situation, "When they first designed the office, we had high hopes for the shower. Everyone said we needed at least two shower stalls since many of the employees would be biking and running to and from work. We're a technology company with lots of young, energetic people, so it made sense."

"I think our CEO, Red, used it once the first week we moved in, after a quick lunchtime run. He made a big deal about it, walking around the office in his sweaty clothes for a good while. He hasn't run since. No one has."

Programmer Chris Duffy, whose cube sits adjacent to the new utility and storage center/closet, nodded and added: "People just started putting crap in the shower — old monitors, boxes, food wrappers... there wasn't room anywhere else, I guess. I took the giant bottle of Prell last month — hate to see that go to waste."

Superstein added, "The shower was hip and humanizing in a way, but converting it makes more sense from a square-inchage [sic] perspective."

Just a month earlier, OviTech Solutions had converted its "gym" room — which consisted of a stationary bike, a treadmill, two Thighmasters and a Abrocker — into a new sales office, retrofitted with eight space-saver cubes. The gym equipment was offered to the employees at cost plus 10 percent. No takers.

Business News

Woman 'Working from Home' Sends Strategically-Timed Emails, Fools No One

"Let's see, Wendy sent a completely meaningless email around 9:30 am, cc'ing the whole marketing team. We should expect an equally mean-ingless and bothersome email around 11ish," said Marsha Petersen, a coworker of Wendy Messermen.

"Wendy works from home quite a lot, and she sends emails every couple of hours to prove she's actually being productive. Must be a pain typing in the old iPhone while you're on the stair climber at the gym, driving to the shore or hitting the sale racks at Bloomingdales."

"It's pretty obvious she's not working," said marketing assistant Doug Barry. "All her emails just ask trivial questions she already knows the answer to, or inquires about the status of something."

"It's never like, 'Here's the analysis of the latest sales figures,' or 'I've finally finished your performance review, what else do you need?' That would be actual work. I usually just wait a half hour to respond because I know she's out the door as soon as she sends it."

"Why can't we just be honest? When I get to work from home... one day, I hope... I'll just send an email to all with the subject line: 'Playing *Gears of War* all day, with an occasional masturbation break, don't you dare interrupt me.'"

Satish Is Pretty Certain Glen Will Die on the Toilet

"Call it really bad luck, but every time I use the bathroom, Glen the sales guy is in the stall next to me making ungodly sounds," reports IT consultant Satish Patel from the safe confines of his office. "I honestly believe Glen is going to die on the toilet."

"I was in the loo a couple months ago and I heard some grumbling next to me. I could tell it was Glen by his shiny black wingtips. The frightening murmurs quickly escalated to some serious growls and rapid huffing and puffing. I thought he was joking. But after two minutes, it did not stop. I got out of there quickly. I thought he was having a heart attack," Satish said.

"I quickly returned with Craig, our company's legal counsel — he knows CPR. As we approached the bathroom door, Glen came walking out whistling happily with a newspaper under his arm."

Satish continued, "Craig told me to relax, Glen was just dropping a 'few fat friends off at the lake.' But, I could see beads of sweat trickling down his temple. It was obvious Glen had just stared the Grim Reaper in the face and barely escaped."

A few minutes later, Rich from marketing ran out of the bathroom holding his nose while gasping, "I think someone just had a shit-balloon fight in stall two, DO NOT go in there!"

A few days later, the unsavory scene repeated itself. Glen was in his favorite stall, exerting tremendous energy trying to move his unyielding bowels. But the knotted fecal impaction wadded in his colon was clearly winning the battle of the butt.

Glen was coaching himself for about three straight minutes, pleading in a strained whine, "Come on boy, let her rip, come on, please... please Lord... come on out... Jesus effing Christ, just come the eff out you little pieces of shit!"

Unfortunately, Satish just happened to be in the adjacent stall again, front and center for the truly disgusting porcelain performance. "I was very scared, yet I could not move. I was paralyzed with the need to know what was going to happen to Glen," said a visibly upset Satish.

"Suddenly, I heard a rapid succession of giant splashing sounds followed by, 'Thank you Jesus, thank you, thank you, sweet Lord!' Then an insidious waft of stink hit me like a turd slingshot to the face. I saw some water hit the floor from the massive displacement. I let out a shriek and sped out of the bathroom without washing my hands. I heard Glen saying 'Hey, who's there... everything's cool... don't worry dude...'"

Feeling even better about his semi-healthy, vegetarian lifestyle, Satish reflected.

"Glen is in very bad shape. He eats two McGriddles for breakfast every morning, Big Macs for lunch every day, smokes cigars, drinks only coffee and scotch, and watches VH1 shows, you know, real vile behavior."

"I feel like I should say something to him, but it's kind of awkward and we're really not that good of friends. Actually, he might be better off if he dies... we all would... especially the poor cleaning people."

Teen Refuses to Admit His 12-Pack is Skunked

"Dude, I've downed four so far and I'm feeling fine," pleaded 15-year-old St. Rose High School sophomore Rich Leahy to a room full of friends. "So don't be a bunch of wusses and just have one! Christ Almighty…"

Rich is referring to a four-month-old Michelob Winter Sampler 12-pack of bottles that he unearthed and brought to Riordan's basement. Despite the allure of alcohol and its liberating effects, his friends wanted nothing to do with Rich or his corroding carton of stinky beers.

"They are not, and I repeat, ARE NOT skunked!" Rich continued his rant as his friends tried their best to ignore him. "Look dude, I buried them under some leaves behind my garage last Christmas Eve after Ray and I swiped them from Quinn's parents party, remember? That was so sweet."

Rich twisted off the cap of another green, red and silver holly-and-snowflake-labeled bottle, oblivious to the malodorous miasma that quickly enveloped the room. "Listen, Indians in Canada used to bury all kinds of stuff — food, wine, corn, newborns — in the ground all winter long for safekeeping, and they were fine. Right? So why the hell would we get sick? Now drink up... chop chop!"

A slightly inebriated Rich continued as he pointed to his trove of beloved, well-aged beers. "All I know is that these little fellas had a nice long winter's nap and now they are ready to party! So someone just shut the hell up and freakin' drink one with me... NOW!"

"Rich can be such a retard! Every time he comes over he tries to get us to drink something disgusting," said friend Tracey Maloney. "Last month he chugged a whole bottle of vermouth he took from my dad's stash. I've never seen so much puke come out of a person so quickly. Sad to say, he was drinking again about twenty minutes later."

"The guy just loves drinking.... anything with alcohol he'll drink it. I saw him cry once when someone stole his Rolling Rock bottle opener," added host Phil Riordan.

After an hour of fruitless enticement and no takers, a sickly greenish tint began to cover Rich's face. Defeated, but not done, Rich grabbed his dank, dirty, leaf-covered carrier and its remaining clanging bottles and headed out to the patio. "You know bro, my grandma used to say, 'Waste not, want not.' I'm sure there are some starving and thirsty kids somewhere in Africa or Bradley Beach who would kill for one of these bad boys." Rich continued on, talking to no one in particular.

Free Band Names!

- ♦ **Weak Need** - taken by an alternative rock band from Texas.

- ♦ **Defying Physics** - taken by a Christian rock band from Iowa.

- ♦ **On The Mend** - taken by an acoustic praise worship artist from IL.

- ♦ **Let's Get Shy** - taken by a guy/girl country band from NC.

- ♦ **You're Really Terrific, But...** - taken by a punk band from London.

- ♦ **Phive Alarm Phire** - taken by a electronic/techno band from VA.

- ♦ **Cathartic Monkeys** - taken by alt-rock band from RI.

Listless Effort

Make the Best of Your Staycation!

Sorry, kids, no Disney this year. How about a staycation?

"Staycation" is a grim word. It reminds us our economy is deeply clogged in the crapper and our savings account is filled with pennies, tumbleweeds and broken dreams. It's also a very lame word to say. You should only use it if you're a coffee-cup-holding, morning TV host giving travel tips and trading barbs with that talkative tub Al Roker.

If you have to partake in one of these gas-saving, budget vacays at least try something a little different... with a much more descriptive name. Here are some suggestions:

Amwaycation - Spend the week with your friends and attempt to sell them crap they don't need!

Aaaycation - Spend the week wearing a leather jacket, punching jukeboxes, courting twins and busting on Potsie!

Beretcation - Spend the week dressed up like Rerun, trying to jump in the back of moving vehicles with the help of your nerdy buddies!

Checation - Spend the week inciting a revolutionary overthrow of other people's vacations!

Cirque du Soleilcation - Spend the week with your kids dressed in leotards and heavy makeup performing extremely dangerous stunts with absolutely no training!

Come Sail Awaycation - Spend the week rocking out to classic Styx (pre-Mr. Roboto only)!

Disobeycation - Spend the week letting the kids do very bad things: cursing, fighting, talking back, even blogging!

Dorian Graycation - Spend the week getting Botox injections on a different body part each day!

Duvetcation - Spend the entire week in bed, blasting the AC and hiding under your comforter from the cruel cruel world outside!

Flambécation - Spend the week experimenting with alcohol and fire in your own little "Myth Busters" home workshop!

Gaycation - Spend the week watching wrestling!

Kid 'n Playcation - Spend the week hosting a house party, showing off your new hi-top fade haircut and quickly fading into oblivion!

Michael Baycation - Spend the week mindlessly blowing shit up and filming it!

Monetcation - Spend the week giving the impression you're having fun!

Rachael Raycation - Spend the week cooking and eating a massive amount of really bad food!

Replaycation - Spend the week watching old vacation movies and reenacting them in your house!

Toupeecation - Spend the week wearing synthetic hair, try a different rug or wig each day!

Karate Helps Kids Focus... on Kicking Ass!

Sorry soccer! Kicking a leather ball is fun, but it's just not challenging enough for the majority of today's high-spirited suburban scamps. Many well-to-do parents see karate, the ancient Japanese practice of self-defense, as a great way for their kids to "focus their attention and boundless energy."

"Our little Noah was quite a handful. He always had a lot of energy and didn't take well to the organized sports we put him in. He was very aggressive and seemed to fight with the others. You know how kids are!" laughs Adam Shapiro.

"So we put him in this karate class our friends recommended, and now he is a totally different child. He loves karate class and can't wait to come home and show us his latest moves. It's really cute!"

"Sometimes he's so focused on his moves, he doesn't realize he's repeatedly battering his little sister in the head with flying roundhouse kicks."

"Oh, and sometimes, the dog or a neighborhood kid will get in the way while Noah's practicing and walk right into one of his larynx-crushing karate chops. But Noah doesn't get distracted, God bless him. He just keeps on practicing. We're very proud!" beams mom Judy, who drives him to his hour-long practices every Tuesday, Wednesday and Friday.

A Visit to Practice

On the way to practice, a silent Noah plays video games ("Hitman: Blood Money") and downs a 20-ounce Coke in the backseat of the family mini-van as Judy explains her son's amazing concentration. "Look at him! He is so into everything he does now. I guess you call it being 'in the zone' or some zen-like thing."

Judy continues to beam proudly while Noah pipes up occasionally. Staring blankly at the monitor built into the back of the driver-side headrest and furiously pounding the game controller with his tiny hands, Noah grumbles, "Die, you jerk!" or "Why won't you die?"

As we enter the Double Dragon Karate Center, we are greeted by Noah's instructor. Pete Visich, karate teacher and bouncer at a local night club, describes the martial art as a great way for kids to get in shape and deal with others. "I teach kids how to fight so they will never have to." When I told him I didn't really understand what he meant. He gladly clarified.

"Come on, you know, Mr. Miyagi said something like it in 'The Karate Kid.' Basically, if you teach a kid how to fight and the others know he can kick some serious ass, then no one will bother him. It's that simple. Hey, want me to show you how to break someone's jaw?" I declined and went over to see how young Noah was doing.

In between kicks, the sweating 5-year-old excitedly shouted, "In soccer, you only get to kick the ball, and in baseball you only get to kick the catcher when nobody is looking. Karate is better because you can kick and punch the other kids all you want and nobody makes you stop or gets mad. It's way cool!"

Adam added, "Noah loves everything about karate. He's got a bunch of different outfits, headbands, belts and accessories. We just ordered him some Chinese throwing stars, nunchakus and tonfas he wanted. I don't know what they are, but they sound like fun!"

Prince Hooks Up with Fat Chick — Roomies Rejoice

Prince William's latest extracurricular activity was all the buzz in the St. Andrews College canteen on Friday morning. Seems the heir to the British throne spent Thursday afternoon blowing off classes and enjoying a major piss-up, downing a case of Carlsberg with his roomies. As the day turned into night, the drinking continued, ending with the sexy scion bedding down a big gal.

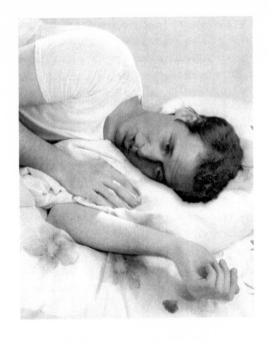

"The bloke was completely aled up... slaughtered... ramped... bladdered!" said Preston Chadwick, Prince William's roommate. "We polished off a bit of the bitters, then broke out the cognac. After we were thoroughly lubricated, the guv'nor was hell bent on getting some rumpy pumpy. He kept yelling, 'Let's go hoggin' mates! Wee Willy and I fancy some some royal action!' So we headed over to this party."

"Normally, Wills is a smarmy geezer who has his way with the ladies at the uni, mostly Page 3 type girls, but last night he was arse-over-tit. He wanted a bit of skirt, but ended up with a bit of rough, if ya know what I mean. He found himself a Sharon and Tracy who was hard on the scales and the eyes," reports Martin Chigglesworth, the Prince's other roomie. "She wasn't one for leaving any bangers on the plate."

"He asked me and Preston if she was dishy. We did our best to suppress our laughter and told him she was a looker and he should definitely roger the bird! 'Go for it Mate!' we said and ushered him off. It was brilliant... the mutt's nuts!."

"Last we saw the knackered bastard, he gave us a big smile, let out a stuffy puff and marched the beastly minger to the nearest bedroom to slip her a length."

Walk of Shame

The next morning, as his roomies were heading to the buttery for some grub, they spotted the randy royal stumbling out of the girls' dorm.

"He was wearing one of her jumpers because he must have honked all over his. It was a bit odd to see him walking, usually he calls for his horse and carriage to pick him up," said Preston.

Martin added, "He looked a bit dicky. When he approached us, he told us to fuck off. It was grand! We hadn't had this much fun since his brother Harry visited. We put glue in his alan whickers when he was sleeping and he had shave off his short and curlies!"

Free Band Names!

- **Acid vs. Bass** – taken by a death metal band from California.

- **The Burning Wick Kids** - taken by ska/alt band from Pittsburgh.

- **Strap In and Begin** - taken by a rock/blues/classic band from Ohio.

- **The Course of Human Events** - taken by a goth metal band from OK.

- **Everything + Everywhere** - taken by an emo screamo band from NY.

- **The Old College Try** - taken by an eight-piece ska band from WI.

- **Would Ya?** - taken by a girl punk band from California.

- **American Goth Itch** - taken by a goth metal band from New Mexico.

- **Beet Keepers** - taken by a screamo, post hardcore band from Texas.

- **These Slacks Fit Nice** - taken by an indie experimental band from TX.

Education News

Education News

MIT Now Offers Poker Major

"I was going to college just to get the hell out of my house so I could play online poker 18 hours a day," said Mike Chung, a poker major who is simultaneously playing three hands of Texas Holdem on three different monitors in his MIT campus dorm room. "When I heard MIT offered poker as a major, I was like 'Hey Cal Tech, you and your aerospace scholarship can suck it, I'm hitting the East Coast to make some mad money!"

Chung, who scored a perfect 1600 on his SATs, and other brilliant young minds like him have traded in their 9-to-5 engineering job aspirations and have immersed themselves in the popular card game. With televised tournaments propelling amateurs to the top of the sport and online betting only a laptop and parent's credit card away, mega-brain students have put fresh air, socializing and general hygiene on the back burner to master this resurgent pastime and begin an exciting new career.

"This is awesome! I just switched majors from cancer research to poker," said a very confident sophomore Randy "Nut Flush" Wertz. "I would usually miss about half of my classes and still ace every exam, but now if I miss a class, I might miss some crucial tips on how to avoid a bad beat from guest lecturers like Phil Gordon, Doyle Brunson, Phil Ivey and that old celebrity chick with the huge rack."

"Just this morning, in my Advanced Raising class, I had 5/5 and was heads-up against an Ace-King off suit. I was thinking the AK must be slightly ahead if 8/9 is ahead versus the 3/3. But I was wrong, my 5/5 was ahead, but only slightly as a 55% favorite. Man, I should have known that!"

"Times change and we try to keep up," said the dean of MIT's Sloan School of Management, Garvin Werner. "We're in tune enough to know the majority of our kids are playing poker online or with friends about 80% of the time, so why not help them instead of pretending it's not happening? We're really proud of this new major. Our school bookstore now has a large section devoted to poker videos and gaming gear. It's very popular." Werner added with a grin as he tipped his black "Shut Up and Deal" cap.

"We set up our own mini-casinos on campus," Werner continued. "Due to the rapid expansion of the Poker Department, we pared back less popular majors and have converted a couple rooms once used for artificial heart research and robotics. Our casinos are very realistic. We pump in stale air, offer an outrageously bland buffet and make the students bet with their own money so they can appreciate the real highs and lows of big stakes poker," Werner added as he motioned to a pair of ATM machines in the front of the room.

Asked if he or the faculty had a problem taking students' betting money in addition to their tuition, Werner replied, "It's nice added revenue for the school, and it's not like our men's basketball team is bringing in a hundred grand a month for us."

"We do use the some of earnings to enhance the program. This past semester, we hired a staff of cocktail waitresses trained to feed the students drinks at a rapid pace and other work-study students hover around the tables in sweat suits, chain smoke and offer unwanted advice. Again, this helps the student deal with real-world situations."

"I'm up a few hundred dollars this month," said a visibly tired Wertz with large bags under his eyes as he constantly flipped a chip between his fingers. "But I'm no fish, there are a bunch of donkeys in my class who are a good 5 to 10 grand in the hole, always playing their beer hands instead of dumping them. Freaking mushes!" Wertz then finished his thought and quickly dashed off to sell some blood plasma to help further fund his education.

In addition to standard poker classes like Gambling Theory, Bluffing and Semi-Bluffing, Psychology of the Trap, Recognizing Tells, Mastering Percentages, Trash Talk and How to Dress Like a Degenerate, the curriculum includes the classics: Card Counting, Sleight of Hand, Grifting, False Cutting and Peek Like a Pro. And while poker is basically a single-player game, the school offers courses like Tournament Play Collusion, Group Scams and Let's Bring Down The Casino to help students bond and work as a group. "We teach these skills so the students can recognize them of course, not actually use them," explained Werner. "We strive to uphold the game's honorable tradition."

A few courses in first aid, wound stitching and how to take a punch are also encouraged as electives for those unfortunate times when the pit bosses confuses you for a cheater and take you to a private meeting with casino security.

Free Band Names!

- **us - you = me** - taken by a three-person Emo/Punk band from MI.

- **What a Thief Believes** - taken by a hardcore band from England.

- **Vandroids** - taken by a goth rock band from England.

- **Conduct Unbecoming** - taken by a melodic metal band from TX.

- **Ambervision** - taken by a punk rock band from Ontario, Canada.

- **Superimposed** - taken by a five-piece giggle girl band in Ohio.

- **The Loudsies** - taken by a four-piece noise band from Washington.

- **News at 11!** - taken by a indie band from Newcastle, Australia.

- **Emboldened** - taken by heavy metal thrash band from Kentucky.

- **Vinolents** - taken by indie/experimental band from Florida.

Unintentionally Gay Music Videos

If you're a "I wish I was young again" person like me and find yourself watching a lot of VH1 Classics, you may have noticed a few things about your favorite vids that were not so apparent when you first viewed them.

Back in the heyday of MTV some established rock acts made a genuine attempt to be innovative with their videos, trying to break the mold of chintzy special effects, testosterone-filled clichés and the perfunctory live performance. Striving to be completely different, some videos turned out, shall we say, just a bit gay. By "gay" of course, we mean every conceivable meaning of the word. Here are some gems:

"Rock Me Tonite" - Billy Squier

http://youtube.com/watch?v=fR0j7sModCI

This classic clip is hands down the most flamboyantly fabulous rock video ever made. And easily the most hysterical. In addition to stroking on stage with a bunch of guys, Billy liked to wind down alone in cozy pink and white sherbet-colored PJs from the Richard Simmons collection. Once comfortable and feeling the need to express himself, the naughty little rock star snaps and prances and writhes around his fancy, silk-strewn bedroom, tossing off pouty glances and come-hither looks to you... and only you... the lucky viewer. Rock him tonite (sic), won't you?

"Hot Rockin'" - Judas Priest

http://youtube.com/watch?v=ki3TpFZY7cU

Four fifths of the band didn't realize this was going to be incredibly gay. One fifth most certainly did. This low-budget video opens with a pack of pasty, leather-and-skin-clad Brits lifting tiny weights in a cramped gym. No argument, this is the most homo-erotic opening ten seconds ever filmed for a heavy metal video. What exactly is Rob Halford doing bobbing up and down? I don't think the skinny chap has the strength to actually pull-off a push-up. Like every Priest video of the era, I loved it... and had no clue Rob was trying to tell us something, despite the not-so-subtle flames engulfing his feet and microphone in the final scene.

73

"Desert Moon" - **Dennis DeYoung**

http://youtube.com/watch?v=Uqjwt8qXjKc

This video should be called "Man Hugs." The Styx's frontman stars in this failed attempt at a macho, male bonding reunion. There's just way too many guys embracing, high-fiving, leering and tackling (shirts-vs-skins football game) to be believable. To be fair, Henry Rollins, Danzig and the guys from GWAR couldn't make this production look hetero. A brief moment showing Mr. Roboto pining away for a lost love (a woman) is not the least bit convincing. He's back to the merry manly hijinks and back-slapping in no time.

"Dancing In The Dark" - **Bruce Springsteen**

http://www.youtube.com/watch?v=mGgC-hPDAUY

After years of being a scrawny and smelly Jersey dirtbag, Bruce was extremely excited to show off his freshly-shaved mug and newly toned biceps. When chirping out a lightweight piece of pop fluff like this, The Boss knew a crisp white blouse with rolled-up sleeves, neatly tucked high into his tight, tight jeans would be the perfect outfit to sway back and forth uncomfortably and attract a whole new audience. Adding to the overall gay motif, the gal he brings up on stage (yes, I know it's the *Friends* chick) has a boy's haircut, boy's clothes and resembles an even cuter Jake Gyllenhaal. And please don't overlook clap-happy Clarence looking like a bouncer at a tranny bar.

"Dancing in the Street" - **Mick Jagger and David Bowie**

http://youtube.com/watch?v=7y-x2fWKbmo

Two rock legends have never — ever — come closer to a full-on make-out session on film than these two sprightly, dancing fools belting out a truly atrocious song. This silly, over-saturated video from 1985 gave fuel to the fire that the Rolling Stone front man and The Thin White Duke were bunk mates back in the day.

"Say Say Say" - **Michael Jackson and Paul McCartney**

http://www.youtube.com/watch?v=iU9OoCyFfr0

I know, this is too easy. Anything with Jacko in it should rule out the word "unintentional," but when Mac and Jack shave and apply make-up together, well, we just can't leave this tender moment alone. Love seemed to be in the air between these pop stars and Linda could do nothing but helplessly watch the romance blossom (and look unsexy strumming a guitar). This otherwise charming and innocent video does contain some serious creepiness; I'm pretty sure the girl Jacko ogles unconvincingly throughout the video is actually his sister La Toya. Ick.

"Lick It Up Video" - Kiss

http://www.youtube.com/watch?v=PzmqgLmCzNQ

When you get past the costumes, the bravado and the fire-spewing theatrics, and just listen to the music, I mean really listen to the music; you'll realize one thing... "Man, Kiss sucked!" That's beside the point. I think this was one of the first videos these jokers did without their theater makeup, (who knows, who cares), but the amount of Mary Kay cosmetics they cake on in its place is visually stunning. Check out the generously applied blush on Paul Stanley's cheek. Cease typing your angry emails Kiss Army members, we know the boys and especially Gene are 100% lady-loving sex machines, he's made a career of telling all about his conquests. What a dork. This video is more of a fashion show catwalk, with the boys ignoring the fawning girls and proudly stating, "Look at our outfits, behold our pretty scarves!"

"Kokomo" - Beach Boys

http://www.youtube.com/watch?v=TvPDB9hDsos

"Hey Beach Boys, wanna do a song for a movie starring that macho hunk Tom Cruise?"

"You bet!"

"Great, you'll love it! It's about bars and drinking and chicks..."

"Tubular! We're so stoked!"

Fast forward two months... Mike Love tucking his unbuttoned shirt into his high-pocket slacks, John Stamos wearing a pink tank top gently tapping some silly bongos and the ambiguously gay Tom Cruise preparing mass quantities of girly drinks made darn sure this classic video is forever filed under "Super Gay!" And no, the bikini-clad chicks running and bouncing down the beach does not make it any less gay.

"Good Vibrations" - Marky Mark

http://www.youtube.com/watch?v=UnzgNAzquCw

We get it, Marky, you work out... a lot... with home-made weights. (What, you couldn't find a Bally's in Boston?) Many male artists have gone shirtless in videos and that's cool, because most of them are pale, flabby messes (Ozzy) or drugged-out, heroin skinny flyweights (that jailbird from STP) and it's a hoot to watch. But when you go shirtless and you are built like a brick shithouse, well that's just gay (read: very intimidating to hetero guys). Let's recap: Musicians who work out and flaunt it: very gay. Musicians who abuse their bodies and flaunt it: very guy.

Free Band Names!

- ◆ **Looks Like Reign!** - taken by Christian rock band from South Africa.

- ◆ **Green Achers** - taken by a Bluegrass band from Arkansas.

- ◆ **The Bossyboots** - taken by a three-piece punk band from NC.

- ◆ **Gadgets Made from Wood** - taken by a punk band from England.

- ◆ **The Exorcissies** - taken by a screamo hardcore band from CA.

- ◆ **Settled for Less** - taken by a kick ass emo/screamo band from NY.

- ◆ **Read My Hips** - taken by a female ska, punk band from Hawaii.

- ◆ **In Droves** - taken by a hard rock band from Wigan, England!

- ◆ **Mise en Garde** - taken by a hip-hop/funk quartet from Australia

- ◆ **Humble Plumbers** - taken by teen girl indie pop band in Minnesota.

- ◆ **The Sun-Drenched Suck-Ups** - taken by pop/rock girl band.

- ◆ **That Less than Fresh Feeling** - taken by Justin from KY.

- ◆ **Dark Sky Parks** - taken by were an alt pop punk band from UK.

- ◆ **Rejection Seat** - taken by Kasey from Zeeland, MI.

Local News

Broken Stop Sign No Match for 9-person Streets Department Work Crew

Broken stop signs don't just fix themselves. It takes a well-oiled machine firing on all cylinders to get the job done. You need the right tools, expert planning, unflagging dedication and in the city of Philadelphia, at least eight members of their Public Works Streets Department crew.

With a solid six hours scheduled for the repair work (and a few extra hours figured in for unforeseen problems), the Philadelphia Street Department deployed a team of nine hardhat-clad workers and three large city trucks to the tony suburb of Chestnut Hill where the malfunction-

ing street sign resided on a quiet side street at a four-way stop intersection. Crew chief Mack Colcannon assessed the situation after thoroughly scoping out the traffic hazard for three hours the day before.

"It looks bad, dangerous, to say the least," said Colcannon as he sipped coffee and pointed to the sign. "When the top bolt falls out, the stop sign swings freely and ends up upside down pivoting on the bottom screw. This is not acceptable and must be fixed immediately, well, as soon as the paperwork passes through the bureau and gets approved, usually within 3 to 5 weeks."

After a 30-minute game-plan meeting, the crew began working at 9:00 am and placed traffic cones and large orange "Men Working" signs at both ends of the street, blocking the road and rerouting the morning traffic. "Safety first," said Colcannon as he looked up from his Daily News sports section from the front seat of his truck.

Work progressed slowly but methodically with each worker — from the four flagmen directing the scant traffic away from the road to the three "spotters" who made sure the "ladderman" was safe as he ascended the three rungs to reach the top of the sign — who made sure the job got done correctly with no mishaps.

"It's physically tough, but rewarding work," said spotter Bill Lambe. "And important! I mean would my boss, his two superiors and the Streets Department Regional Director spend all morning standing around drinking coffee and watching us if this wasn't an important job? I don't think so." Lambe excused himself as he and the rest of the crew boarded their trucks and headed to a Wawa for their union mandated "morning break" (10:30 am-10:50 am).

After a solid and successful early afternoon of attacking the problematic sign head on, and getting it back in its upright position, the team encountered a roadblock. Even with lots of planning and skill, some jobs pose unique and unexpected challenges that can delay a timely completion.

"We brought the wrong bolt," said Colcannon as he hopped in his truck and left to get the correct replacement after a quick team meeting.

Work may have halted for an hour or so, but the team took the time to rest up and re-energize (some napped under a large elm tree while others took refuge in the cab of their trucks) to prepare for the final leg of work.

Many workers are content to put in their 37.5 hours a week and collect a check. Many more would stop right at 4:35 pm (the official end of day for these union workers) and leave their work until the next day. Not this plucky bunch.

With the sign half fixed at the closing bell, these dedicated professionals stayed the extra two hours to finish the job and put in the necessary overtime to get the job done right. The overtime pay of twice their regular hourly rate was scant compensation for delaying their happy hour stop at Towey's Tavern, and thus pushing back even further their return to wives, children and homes.

Sports News

Local Boy Wears Filthy Baseball Uniform for Entire Weekend

Eleven-year-old Jason McCarthy put on his freshly laundered Allendale Pirates Little League uniform Friday at 7:30 a.m. and proudly wore it to school for their annual "Sports Day." Despite the rapid accumulation of dirt, sweat, food stains and various body and animal odors, the sixth-grade shortstop wore it for 58 straight hours without once giving a thought to changing into something else.

After school, McCarthy headed directly to the playground for tackle football with friends followed by pizza and videos at his home. Ignoring pleas from his mother, the dirt-clad boy did not wash before bed or change into his jammies. Waking up late in his soiled uniform, he rushed to the local ball field to join his team for the first double-header of the season. Following a day filled with diving catches and sliding stolen bases, Jason celebrated with large dripping chili dogs and grape juice, most of which did not end up in his mouth. He then went directly to his friend's house to spend the night.

The boys played manhunt in the woods until 9:00 pm and then wrestled with the neighbor's St. Bernard for another hour. McCarthy then retired to bed without stepping out of his clothes or thinking about a toothbrush. He spent all Sunday afternoon building a tree fort. "I noticed he did not bring a change of clothes, so I asked if he wanted to borrow some of Bobby's," said his friend's mother. "He said, 'No way, that's gay!' so I let him be."

Cancer con Carne

"Molto Mario" Batali, rotund celebrity chef on the Food Network, has been diagnosed with cancer of the fat. An enormous malignant tumor the size of a mortadella salami was found in a large tuft of fat sitting on top of the corpulent cook's abdominal region. The tumor was removed after an eight-hour surgery, sautéed with asparagus and capers, and served with a 1997 Woodward Canyon Cabernet Sauvignon.

Batali's doctor said it will takes weeks to check the rest of the fat to see if the cancer has spread. He remains optimistic in his prognosis, "The cancer has a hard time penetrating the dense layers of butter and cheese that make up about 70% of most chefs' body fat."

Batali blames the cancer on an experimental vegetarian period of his life, "I think the cancer snuck in my body back in college when I only ate carrots, corn and Snickers. My body's natural defenses were weak... I had no meat, which I believe is an anti-carcinogen, to fight off the disease."

Free Band Names!

- ♦ **Mixed Meta 4** - taken by a hard core rock band from AK.

- ♦ **Jarring Hit** - taken by a punk group from Nebraska.

- ♦ **The Facelifters** - taken by an emo/rock band from Michigan.

- ♦ **Chimptronic** - taken by a rock pop band from England.

- ♦ **Words to the Song** - taken by a emo/punk band from IN.

- ♦ **These Bruising Stones** - taken by emo/goth band from UK.

- ♦ **The Darwinistas** - taken by a rock band from Brunei, SE Asia.

- ♦ **Ginormous** - taken by a versatile rock band from India.

- ♦ **Flee Collar** - taken by a hip-hop rock band from Australia.

Freshman Starts Scrabble Club, Gains Instant Popularity

In an attempt to make friends at his new school, Leo Jeffries started a Scrabble Club. The skinny, 14-year-old freshman was shocked to find out that an esteemed learning institution like Elmont High School did not already have a Scrabble club.

Within a day of posting 50 bright yellow "Do You Dabble in Scrabble?" flyers in the hallways, over 100 enthusiastic students signed up for the fledgling club.

"I was so excited to meet all these cool people! There is a great mix of kids in the club... jocks, cheerleaders, student body officers and lots of other popular kids. I never knew there were so many people into Scrabble word games, anagrams and etymology. It's great! I even met a really nice girl and we are going on a date this Saturday night. I can't wait..."

Sadly, the ebullient Leo is rudely interrupted mid-sentence by the blaring morning alarm clock of reality that awakens the confused lad and end yet another dream that will never, ever come true.

Tonight on Your Local News!

Ferocious Lions Breeding in Your Backyard?

- Inventor Kid Invents Useless Piece of Crap!

- Americans Look Forward to Not Giving a Shit about Olympic Swimming for another Four Years!

- Disturbing Hidden Camera Footage Reveals Local Health Club Still Playing Fabulous Thunderbirds Videos!

- 'Real World' Cast Member Dies During 'Gauntlet' Event, Doctor Determines Cause of Death to Be *Old Age*!

- Bush Orders Google to Turn Over Data for Waldo Searches!!

- $400 in Singles Later, Man Still Thinks He Has a Pretty Good Shot with Stripper!

- Next on 'Lost': Entire Episode Devoted to Sawyer's T-Shirt's Backstory!

- Cast Member from 'The Hills' Admits, 'It's So Like, Um, You Know.'

- New iPod Scheduled for Release the Day After You Buy a New One!

- Pope Fakes Illness So He Can Catch Up on His E-mails!

- Local Centaur Tired of Giving Everyone Rides!

- Oprah Audience Laughs Hysterically Once Again for No Apparent Reason!

- Tests Find Glazed, Blueberry Bagel to Be a Donut!

- Man Deems Furniture Rental a 'Scam' after Spending $7,000 on Loveseat over Two Year Period!

- Weather Channel Scientists Close to Perfecting Giant Hurricane Generating Machine!

- Hurricane Victims Plead for Relief from Geraldo Rivera!

- "Unofficial" Wendy's Spokesman Has "Official" Massive Heart Attack!

- REM's Bass Player Braces for Another Round of Harry Potter Jokes!

- 'Extreme Makeover: Home Edition' Builds New Robot Parents for Orphans!

- Parents Around the World Fear Britney Spears Will Give Her Baby the Same Name as Their Child!

- Man Stuck in Bathroom Stall for 20 Extra Minutes Waiting for Pee Stain to Dry!

- Amazon Reviewers Now Able to Review Other Reviewers' Reviews!

- Tired from Running, Sasquatch Agrees to Sit-down Interview!

- Wedding Photographer's Tux Celebrates 30th Birthday!

- Oprah Pledges to Dispense Weight Loss Advice on a Daily Basis Until She Gets Fat Again!

- NHL Players Now Free to Spend More Quality Time with Their Massive Concussions!

- Ugly Teens Support Accurate Portrayal on "Joan of Arcadia!"

- Man Standing in Empty Living Room Filled with Food, Drinks and Party Decorations Suddenly Realizes His MySpace Friends are Not Actually His Real Friends!

Sedentary Teens Flock to Eating Clubs and Competitions

Due to student demand, Midvale High in Walling Township, NJ, and other schools across the nation have added Competitive Eating to their roster of school-sponsored clubs.

The goal of the new and extremely popular intramural "sport" is simple. The participant (eater) attempts to ingest as much food as possible within a certain time period without throwing up or choking. The participant who eats the most wins.

The clubs are based on the Nathan's Famous Hot Dog Eating Contest held on Coney Island every year, where contestants try to eat as many hot dogs (buns plus meat) as they can in a 12-minute judged competition. This event and others like it have gained popularity as the menus have expanded from hot dogs to chicken wings, ribs, matzo balls, steaks, Asian noodles, pizza, brisket, Klondike bars, tripe, haggis, bull testicles, sheep anuses, and Pez.

The clubs have attracted a wide range of the student population, from youths who normally eschew group athletics in favor of more individual pursuits, to kids who are just plain hungry because of funding cutbacks by the Bush administration.

The afterschool events are sponsored by local and national businesses, which provide the mass quantities of eatables in exchange for marketing rights in the schools. For instance, at Midvale, the gymnasium now bears a sign that reads "Hoagie Shack Presents Hoagieland Hall."

"I was never a fan of team sports, or activities that required you to actually get up from your seat," said Anthony De Carmellio, a well-fed sophomore at Midvale. "I like sports where you don't have to move a lot, like the luge or NASCAR. I tried golf last year because it seemed easy, but they wanted me to get out of the cart before I swung the club. I wasn't into that. So when I heard about this eating club in my school, I jumped right into it. Well not actually jumped, but I eventually got around to signing up a few days later."

"It's really hard work but when you put your mind and mouth to it, anything is possible," commented Adam Fleisher, a bookish junior who definitely knows his way around a fat Italian sausage. "We've got a great squad of seriously motivated eaters, and our coach, Mr. Whitaker the gym teacher, is a really good hands-on instructor and a really good cook," Fleisher continued, after popping a few cool-down frosted donut holes in his mouth and wiping his face with the bottom of his tank top. "I'm a perfectionist, so I am always practicing and upping my intake. To be a top-level athlete, you gotta set goals."

Fleisher's practice session usually includes a heaping platter of boiled frankfurters, a 16-inch meat-lover's pizza, four packs of Ding Dongs and a carton of chocolate milk. He tries to get in a least four practice eating sessions a day, five days a week. On the weekends, he just eats whatever he wants. "I try to set an example for my teammates, so I am usually the first one in and the last one to leave -- the cafeteria, that is."

Midvale school psychologist Betty Ann Davenport believes competitive eating is a positive activity because the team spirit helps with the socialization process: "The majority of cardio-averse teenagers usually spend their free time playing video games, watching TV and eating fast food alone. Outdoor activities requiring physical movement, increased heart rate, perspiring and possible physical harm are not attractive to this sedentary group. But for some of these teens, boredom and monotony set in and they eventually crave new avenues of entertainment and camaraderie, like the competitive eating clubs. For others, it's an extracurricular activity that looks good on their college transcripts!"

"It's exciting. Everyone is really into it and goes crazy when we win an event," Fleisher enthused as he prepared for practice by downing a warm-up package of Pizza Rolls. "It's like when you get to the 97th level of Dungeon Claw III and finally slay Bytor the Morlock with the enchanted broadsword; it's that cool!"

At a recent competition which pitted the Midvale Munchers against their rivals, the Toms River Gorgers, 430-pound Midvale team captain Orandice Jackson walked away with the bean-burrito-eating crown after consuming 30 burritos (each weighing 1 lb.) in 15 minutes and then treating the crowd to some celebratory dancing (and triumphant gas explosions).

Jackson grabbed his trophy and told a reporter for the school newspaper, "First and foremost, I'd just like to thank my savior, the Lord Jesus Christ, for giving me the ability and talent to perform today. And I'd also like to thanks my parents, who taught me to be all I can be and to always finish all my food."

Free Band Names!

- ♦ **Sentenced to Beth** - taken by a singer/songwriter duo from SC.

- ♦ **Shirtz vs. Skinz** - taken by a punk rock band from Louisiana.

- ♦ **Horripilation** - taken by four rocker punk girls from the country, TN.

- ♦ **Just Plain Jealous** - taken by four-piece punk poppers from TN.

- ♦ **12-Step Shuffle** - taken by a screamo hardcore band from Georgia.

- ♦ **The Norfolk Broads** - taken by a punk rock band from Wisconsin.

- ♦ **Four Sons of Horus** - taken by an alt-rock band from New Jersey.

- ♦ **Behold the Clever Tee** - taken by an emo band from PA.

Philly Dog Walker Expands Business to Include Musicians

Vicki Larkin was worried. Her boyfriend Scott seemed depressed. He was sleeping late, acting grumpy and thumbing his nose at any suggestion of exercise or a change to a healthier lifestyle.

Scott plays bass in Cousin Tweedy, a popular Philly-based alt-country band that gigs about three to four times a week. Scott stays up till the wee hours, drinks copious amounts of scotch and rarely sees Vicki, who works during the day as a human resources representative.

"If I was home, I'd make sure he'd get out of the house and eat right," laments a concerned Vicki. "But I can't, so I had to think out of the box for a solution to this problem."

"One day I saw this professional dog walker in our apartment building. Watching how good she was with the doggies and how happy the little guys seemed gave me a great idea. I struck up a conversation with her, and 10 minutes later I scheduled her for four half-hour visits each week with Scott."

Anna Watson has been walking dogs for six years and makes a good living. "I was looking to expand my business. I truly love dogs but they get a bit boring. You know, lots of one-sided conversations. So taking on lonely musicians needing exercise and company sounded very intriguing."

"The first time I went to get Scott, around 11:00 am on a rainy Tuesday, he was a bit timid and groggy. I think he just woke up. But after a little coffee and some playtime together (Guitar Hero, Daily News Jumble), he really perked up and seemed to like me," says Watson. "Now, every time I go to the door, Scott bounds out of his room and greets me very enthusiastically. He keeps jumping up and down until I pat him on the head and give him his favorite treats, a gummy bear and a Marlboro Light. He is so sweet. I'll say 'Does somebody want to get some coffee-woffee?' or 'Who wants to go to the guitar shop and by some new stringy-wingies?' and he'll slobber happily as we prepare to go outside."

Watson recommends taking it slow with housebound musicians. You have to gain their trust. They see most humans as "club-owner" types, who just want to rip them off and not pay them.

When you walk them around the city, they may growl at people who regularly bathe because the soap and deodorants are very foreign to their sense of smell. Sunscreen is also a must before you take them out for a walk. "Many of these nocturnal beings have not been in the sunlight in months and prolonged exposure to its harmful rays could permanently scar their ashen skin."

"I keep a bunch of pieces of old frozen pizza in my pocket to give to Scott as reward for behaving well," beams Watson. "Sometimes when we happen upon another musician on the street, he'll want to play or ask if they got representation or label interest. It's sooooo cute."

Vicki is ecstatic with the results. "Scott is a changed man. He showers almost daily and talks to me for a good 20 minutes before he picks up his guitar and puts on his headphones. Our relationship is definitely heading in the right direction."

"And I just looooove Anna. She is extremely encouraging when he is good, She taught Scott to put his dishes in the sink. And she is very strict with him when he misbehaves. She said he is making good progress with his little peeing on the seat problem and still needs to remind him to get out of bed when he has to puke."

Listless Effort

Olympic Event Enhancements

The Olympics sure are fun to watch, but not every event is as thrilling as it could be. Here are some simple suggestions for improvement:

EVENT	ENHANCEMENT
Gymnastics Floor Exercise	Add celebrity partner
Water Polo	Add jellyfish
Women's Softball	Replace catcher's mitt with hand puppet
Gymnastics Pommel Horse	Add hot butter
Men's Eight Rowing	Change to seven coxswains, one rower
Wrestling	Allow kissing
Beach Volleyball	Add horseshoe crabs
Table Tennis	Add plastic cups and beer
Men's Four-Man Kayak	Change Four-Man to Three-Men-and-a-Baby
Sailing	Add Scylla and Charybdis
Weightlifting	Require roller skates
Diving	Subtract water

EVENT	ENHANCEMENT
Synchronized Diving	Conjoined twins only
Equestrian	Replace dumb outfits with armor
Hammer Throw	Add nails
Women's Judo	Allow hair pulling
Archery	Replace target with apple on head
Soccer	Allow three balls in play at once
Badminton	No shuttle, just cock
Gymnastics Rings	Change to "Rings of Fire"
Rhythmic Gymnastics	Men only
Gymnastics Balance Beam	Add barrel-throwing ape
Trampoline	All competitors compete at once
Mountain Bike	Allow Segways
Fencing	Must dress as pirate

Olympics News

China Calls in Sick to Work

[beep]… "Um, hey (cough cough), I'll be taking a sick day today. It's been a crazy couple of weeks and I put in a lot of serious O.T. with the "big show" and I'm like, just really wiped out, ya know. If I see another firework or drum or that Misty May whatever, I'll seriously hurl… So I'll be laying in bed, probably just catching up on some "Project Runway"… I know, I heard it sucks this season, but whatever… just need to chill. I'll definitely be back in work tomorrow, have a huge backlog of authoritarian suppression that needs to be meted out pronto, plus we have to release the noxious smog back in the air. Anywho… anything urgent, just contact Sudan. Bye."

5K-Run Ruined When Terrorist Wins Race

The participants of the Avalon, NJ, 23rd Annual Memorial Day 5K-Run — proudly donning their official "Terrorism Won't Win" race T-shirts — were extremely dismayed and angered to learn the race was won by a terrorist.

"It's just really disturbing that the theme of our race this year is 'Terrorism Won't Win' and an actual terror-ist came in first. Looks like terrorism did win... and in record time," said Avalon resident Richard Comstock. "Man, and we spent months coming up with that stupid slogan..."

Other slogans considered by the 5K-Run committee were, "These Colors Don't Run," "Zero Tolerance for Terrorists," "No Time for Terror," "Run for America, Not from Terror" and the old standby, "Beer, Its Not Just For Breakfast Anymore."

The winner, Rafiq Hassan, is a member of the Al Qaeda Running Club. The Club's sole purpose (as stated on their website) is, "To defeat all fat, slow Americans in their silly little races and in turn, demoralize the country and bring down the insidious capitalist system. We also wish to stay in shape and get a good cardio workout."

Mike Davies, owner of Colonel Crabbies' Crab Shack, who "ran" the race in 45:23, was very "pissed off" after hearing the news. "This is why we need background checks on runners with Arabian names. It may not seem fair, like what we did to the Chinese in those camps in the Civil War, but hey, it's better to be safe than sorry."

Hassan was very happy with his victory and winning time of 14:57, beating his nearest filthy American competitor by two minutes. "I felt really good out there... nice, fast course. It was a perfect day to run, have fun, praise Allah and wish imminent death to your satanic leader George Bush."

Free Band Names!

- ◆ **The Alien Ate Ed** - taken by an emo/punk band from Missouri.

- ◆ **Meg A. Picks Hell** - taken by a punk band from Utah.

- ◆ **NASDIQ** - taken by an emocore/metal band from CA.

- ◆ **Rough Seize** - taken by a punk rock band from Florida.

- ◆ **High and Tight** - taken by a screamo band from Illinois.

- ◆ **Kentucky Fried Kansas** - taken by a country band in FL.

- ◆ **Shouty** - taken by five-peice screamo band from AZ.

- ◆ **The Tingly** - taken by a ska band from New Mexico.

- ◆ **Our Solar-Powered Son** - taken by rock band from OZ.

- ◆ **Ampliflyer** - taken by a bunch of silly emos from Iowa.

- ◆ **Little Rusty** - taken by rock band 40-year-olds from NY.

- ◆ **Property of** - taken by small punk band in toronto.

- ◆ **Six Solid Reasons to Run** - taken by a punk/rock band from CA.

- ◆ **Temper Temper** - Taken by a band from Harrisburg, PA.

- ◆ **May The Best Man Survive** - taken by a rock band from the UK.

Minor Milestones

Every day milestones are reached but sometimes go unnoticed. Here are some lesser known yet still impressive events we caught using The Wigometer 3000™, our super-powered, pop-culture-detecting radar system.

* **100,000,000th** mundane meal-related status update on Facebook

* **10,000th** fake question posed by a fake reader in Parade magazine

* **1,000th** "Next Big Thing" declared at SXSW/CMJ this year

* **1,000th** time today Kanye West has impressed himself

* **100th** product in your supermarket featuring Rachael Ray's fat face

* **4,000th** spiritual geek matched up with timid nerd on eHarmony.com

* **500th** grainy, dark, out-of-focus surveillance photo made crystal clear with the simple click of a mouse on crime show by snippy female computer whiz

* **3,000,000th** blurry TwitPic photo of someone's salad posted

* **15,000th** Christopher Walken impression done by a hack stand-up comedian

* **25th** episode of "Lost" featuring lots of boring stuff from the past jam packed between two minutes of actual, plot-advancing action

* **45,000th** mention of "Tyra" by Tyra on Tyra's show

* **2,000,000,000th** occurrence of God personally helping an athlete or celebrity win something

* **700th** opportunity seized by Al Sharpton

* **500th** stolen joke updated with the word "beaner" by Carlos Mencia

* **800,000th** personal blog that hasn't been updated since Feb. 2006

* **1,000,000th** stock photo showing a laptop screen pointed at by three ethnically-diverse and smiling business people

* **10th** rebate check actually sent in and payment promptly received

* **5,000,000th** piece of chintzy retro crap bought on eBay by someone who immediately regrets the purchase

* **3,000th** title in the "Dummies" series of books hit the shelf: "Fucking for Dummies"

* **20,000th** day in a row Prince Charles has not had a real job

* **500,000th** deep arterial laceration of a human hand while trying to open a product packaged in that sharp, hard-plastic shrink wrap

* **50,000th** "Goodfellas" poster hung on a Rutgers University dorm room wall

* **3,000,000th** rock-hard erection guaranteed in your inbox

* **1,000th** use of the word "percentile" by your new-parent friend

* **750,000th** spin of "Sweet Child O' Mine" on Philadelphia radio

I Own an Old Person Phone

Looking over my cell phone bill for February, I was not surprised to see I only made three calls, total. All calls were made to my local pizza place on a Friday, to facilitate picking up dinner on my way home from work.

Please note: I made the calls before I started driving. That's how we do it here in Safetyville, Population: 1.

> *"Only three calls, Jeff!" You say incredulously. "Have you no friends? Have you no plans? Have you no uncomfortable moments alone in public where you must call someone, anyone, unnecessarily just to make yourself seem busy or important?"*

True, plans and friends are at a minimum, but when I'm away from my desk and my computer, I need the buzzing, the ringing and the key-tapping to cease. That is why I don't use my cell often or keep it on. I would love not to own one, but I realize my pizza procurement plan would take a hit if I went phoneless.

Luckily, I found the perfect fit for my neo-Luddite, never-busy, never-needed lifestyle in the pages of the latest AARP magazine or Readers Digest, or whatever I was reading in my in-laws bathroom.

The Jitterbug is a phone for seniors: big-ass buttons, bare bones features and a complete lack of nonsense to interfere with making and receiving a call. It is the polar opposite of an iPhone and even the opposite of a budget throw-away celly used by your friendly neighborhood drug dealer.

No frills, no nonsense, affordable, this phone was perfect for me.

Despite my bad knees and constant complaining, I am not a senior. But, I was pleased as punch to find out you do not have to be a senior to get in on this fabulous deal. I immediately ordered one.

Yes, this phone is not for most people, especially if you're a Cingular/AT&T user. The Jitterbug does not have the special feature you've grown to love, the feature that connects you to the internet (and charges you!) every time you mistakenly hit the button you'd think would never ever do such a thing.

It also does not send you emails or phone messages with special offers like many of the providers out there. They all stink—their service and their phones—and I just wanted to free myself of their clutches. I'm glad I did.

Phone Frustration

The piece of shit phone I had prior to my *Love Bug* (I don't call it that, I swear) would not allow me to simply make a call without three or four extraneous clicks. Grrrrr! I'd dial my number or choose it in my 9-clicks-to-get-to Phone Book and then have to hit the center button which would then give me a list of choices:

- Add to Address Book
- Edit Phone Number
- Change your Ringtone
- Add a Ringtone
- Create Your Own Ringtone
- Play a Game
- Watch a Fergie Video
- Fuck Your Mother
- Throw Phone against Wall
- Place Call
- Change Your Plan
- Add Minutes
- Take a Photo

I eventually did throw this piece of useless plastic against the wall. This may sound like I'm a complete idiot, but when I was done with a call and just wanted to "hang up," the goddamn phone would not do so, no matter which button I pressed.

I actually resorted to turning my phone OFF to end a call. Yep, just like your grandma who unplugs her computer every time she is done using it, I would hit OFF because I could not end a simple call. I'm sure I got an excessive OFFing charge every time I did so too.

"Jeff, don't you build websites and keep up with all things tech? How can you be so hapless?"

I am fairly techy, but to me, "phone" technology is the sleazy bottom rung of innovation, where good usability and user experience takes a backseat to the overt stealing of customers' money with hidden fees, insane charges and inscrutable minute plans; all geared to trick you and sap you of your patience and willingness to fight back. If I only make 5 effing calls a month, why is $39.95 the cheapest effing plan I can buy?

You Buggin'? I'm Buggin'!

Okay back to my new giant phone, which I love. It is made for old people and technophobes who are easily confused by the myriad functionality of today's latest cell phones. So, the backwards-thinking engineers at Jitterbug HQ made the phone nice and simple to use, no tricks. It only has:

- Enormous Number Pad
- YES and NO Buttons
- ON/OFF Button
- UP and DOWN Scroller
- Big Soft Ear Cushion
- Bright Screen with Large Text.

No camera, no video, no texting, no taser, no bottle opener, just the basics. Oh, and a jarring jitterbug jingle that play loudly every time you turn it off and on. Want to change the tune? Sorry, not possible. A small concession, I can deal.

I got the "Graphite" model, a little slicker than the orthopedic white, wouldn't you agree? My phone number is also engraved in a large font right under the screen. This is sweet, because I had to tape a post-it with my number on the back of my old phone.

My new phone plan is $15/month for more minutes than I'll use, and the unit cost about $150. It's a *very very large* phone, a two-hander (think Gordon Gecko's mobile phone in *Wall Street*).

For people who want less buttons, there is also a Jitterbug "OneTouch."

It is easily the most dumbed-down piece of phone-tech out there. It gives the user only three options:

- Operator
- Tow
- 911

I guess after exhaustive research, they deemed these three choices the most popular things old people need in a phone.

- Operator – *"Hello, operator, will it be chilly outside today?"*
- Tow – *"Hello, I'm upside down again in my car. Help me."*
- 911 – *"Hello dear, does my friend Bernice have a phone? Can you put me through?"*

The Jitterbug Forum and Customer Service

While I have not been there, I think the Jitterbug User Forum looks something like this:

JITTERBUG USER FORUM - Total Post: 3 (since February 2007)

"Yoohoo… Is anybody there/? I can't find my phone. Help. The kettle is whistling >& I'll be right back oh dear."

"Maddie, Connor, it's Grandma! If you're on the internet and see this please call me, I miss you."

"Hi Ladies, what are you wearing?"

The customer service and online ordering are top-notch. You can call them and they will enter names and numbers in your phone book for you or you can do it online. You can also fax them over the info, which I found odd. I think if a person can't handle a phone, faxing a document successfully might not be in his or her skill set.

The voice that guides you through your set up on the phone sounds just like a caring grandma who knows a thing or two about a thing or two. She goes nice and slowly, gives clear explanations and buys you gifts that don't fit from JC Penney's. She rules.

Functions

So, I basically can:

- Make a Call
- Receive a Call
- Check my Voicemail
- Successfully Hang Up

What else would a boy need?

I played with the iPhone for a bit and it was fun, but after ten minutes I was bored. It reminded me of work. It was just like using a computer, a very small, hard-to-navigate computer. I do enough fat-finger typing on my normal-sized keyboard, this was just silly.

I have a camera that takes great photos and video and is small enough to carry around in addition to my phone. Plus I don't have to compromise on the quality of the photos. Yes, I can't take stealthy, sneaky phone photos of hot, drunk chicks in bars doing slutty things while I pretend to talk. I'll just have you send me your shots instead. Problem solved. Thanks.

> *"What no ringtones in your life, Jeff? How will you let people know your exquisite, indie musical taste if you can't play crappy digitized versions of the songs on your phone?"*

If you buy ring tones, you are either an unsupervised teen girl or a complete ass.

> *"I like my exciting, always linked-in-to-the-grid lifestyle. Eat shit, loser. I definitely won't DIGG this story."*

Alright, calm down. I know this Jitterbug lifestyle is not for everyone, but I sit in front of a computer for about 10+ hours a day and the last thing I need is to do when I'm out of office is check my email while I'm waiting to get my hair cut or taking a walk with my daughter. Or driving. I applaud my home state of New Jersey (and I don't so that often) for going after you jerk-offs who text and talk while attempting to maneuver your vehicles. May your last text be:

> *"OMG… my spine just snapped in half… G2G!"*

Entertainment News

Cameron Crowe Excited about New Soundtrack

"I've been working close to five years on this soundtrack and I think it's my best one to date," said an animated Cameron Crowe discussing his latest music compilation that will accompany his new movie project that has yet to be written or cast.

"This is my life. I'm a soundtrack maker. Nothing gives me more satisfaction than searching for and finding the perfect old classic rock song that says, 'Hey world, look at how much more I know about obscure 70s and 80s music than you do.'"

Crowe, relaxing in his home office wearing a Badfinger t-shirt and listening to Bread's third album "Manna" on his vintage record player, expounded upon his life's love. "It's extremely important to me to find the coolest old rock songs or the latest inoffensive, adult-alternative songs before other soundtrack makers like Quentin Tarantino, Wes Anderson or Sofia Coppola put it on their soundtracks."

Known for his other hit soundtracks *Say Anything*, *Singles* and *Almost Famous*, Crowe spends countless hours digging through indie record stores and going through his own sizeable collection of vinyl. "There's this rare Flying Burrito Brothers song from 1971 that did not make it on any of their albums that I am trying to get the rights to. That will definitely kick off my next soundtrack! I mean, right after the requisite Elton John and Nancy Wilson songs. She's so awesome, have you heard her latest? People love Heart, you know." Crowe asks as he forces a stack of her latest CDs into my hands.

When asked about the new film that accompanies the soundtrack, Crowe was not as enthused as he thumbed through old copies of Cream and Circus magazines he keeps piled on his coffee table. "Films are just something you have to do, you know, to promote the soundtracks and keep the suits at the studios happy."

Local News

Moody Teen and Family Dog Misuse Panic Room

Within six hours of the completion of the Krauss family's new high-security "panic room," the local police were alerted and dispatched to the posh suburban development to answer a call of distress. Steven Krauss commissioned the $120,000 steel-walled addition because he was growing extremely concerned about terrorists.

"You see, I am VP at a very prominent securities firm in New York and believe I might be targeted by terrorists who are looking to destabilize our financial institutions and the economy in general. I've heard these Middle Eastern bad guys are in the process of kidnapping important executives in the industry and their family members," said a very serious Krauss. "I'm not going to let that happen to us."

"So, it made perfect sense to construct a safe room in our house where we could convene in case of a break-in and wait for the police. On paper, it was an excellent idea. Baddies come to our house, we run into the panic room, press a button and we are completely secured in the dynamite-proof room until help arrives. We put in a couple Pottery Barn couches, a TV and some bottled water just in case it takes a while."

The plan did have one major flaw. Krauss did not count on his moody teenage daughter Zoë to seek refuge in the room whenever her parents were, "totally being dickheads!"

Repeat Offender

"Yeah, right after the room was finished, Zoë had one of her little tantrums. Something about us not letting her get cosmetic surgery until she's at least 16," recalled Krauss. "After five minutes of screaming in the kitchen, she grabbed her cell phone, a can of Pringles and tore out of the room. Normally she'll lock herself in her bedroom, blast her music and cool down. But not this time."

Zoë entered the room and immediately chimed in, "If you and Mom are going to act like overbearing ogres, then I need to make a major statement to show you how, like, totally wrong you are! I didn't realize the cops were alerted every time you press that stupid button...whatever... I was just trying to make a point. If you disrespect me, then I'll disrespect you!"

It has been two months since the grand opening of the terrorist-free haven and the mercurial Zoë has locked herself in 13 times — each time requiring a visit from the local police.

"Cut me a break! I only use it when I REALLY need to show them how upset I am. Like when they took away my platinum card because I bought a horse online and...." Zoë ends her defense mid-sentence as she flips on Gossip Girl and completely zones out.

In a phone interview, Sgt. Seymour of the West Chester Police Force elaborated on the growing problem. "Yup, it's getting to be a real pain. About six families in this neighborhood have these stupid ass rooms in their house, and we get these false alarms all the time. What happened to having a freakin' game room? Someone broke into our house when we were kids and we ran into our rec room in the basement, got some pool sticks and beat the piss out of the guy. The cops almost arrested us. I think the guy's a vegetable now."

In the Doghouse

Krauss's wife Mindy tells of another frequent habitant of the new mini fortress. "I guess our dog Winthrop has been watching Zoë tear in and out of the panic room and picked up some bad ideas. At first, he would timidly sniff around the room and just peek his head in. Now he'll just grab a couch cushion, drag it into the panic room, press the button with his front paw and go to town on the cushion. We're helpless to stop him."

"The breeders guaranteed us he was a purebred golden retriever. You know, supposedly a real good dog. We got him at this expensive puppy farm in upstate New York," said Krauss. "He's a purebred alright... a purebred, crazy-ass, furniture-shredding furball!"

Winthrop has tripped the alarm six times.

Parents Join In

"I must say, Mindy and I gathered the family in the panic room the other night because of a possible threat that turned out to be nothing," Krauss continued. "But I was extremely glad we had the opportunity to practice. We all got in the room in under two minutes. It was like a very productive fire drill that..."

Zoë quickly interrupted.

"Duh dad, why don't you tell them what the 'possible threat' really was? Or are you too embarrassed to say you didn't realize our nanny ordered Indian food for dinner and you thought the Indian delivery boy was a terrorist when he showed up at the door?"

"And, even after the police identified him as an employee of the Indian restaurant, you still wanted him brought down to the station and questioned. Huh? Do you mention that, scaredy-pants?"

"Zoë, be quiet and go to your room! And I don't mean the goddamn panic room!!" Krauss screamed as he chased his daughter down the hallway.

Entertainment News

Bruce Willis's Kind Gesture Turns into Night of Horror

Hollywood hotshot Bruce Willis was not only gracious enough to attend his 30th high school reunion; he footed the bill for the entire extravagant soiree at the posh Trump Plaza in Atlantic City. The munificent megastar treated his fellow classmates from Carneys Point High School in New Jersey to a night of fond memories, pricey cocktails, sumptuous dinner, and in a strange turn of events, an unspeakable act of diabolical cruelty.

"Everything was fabulous until we were all escorted into the main theater after dinner to see the band. There was talk that he got Cheap Trick or Styx and we were really pumped up. I don't think anyone was prepared for what happened next," said classmate Marcus Goldman.

"The lights went down and then this really atrocious blues-rock-type crap started blaring from these giant speakers and then these really cheesy gospel singers started flailing their arms and singing. I knew something bad, something evil was coming," said Willis's high school sweetheart Dawn Cromer. "Then Bruce, who had changed into a black skullcap, jeans, and a tight undershirt rode onstage on a motorcycle and started belting out a shitty version of 'Proud Mary,' or something like that. I just froze and felt a cold, dark fear envelope the room."

Bring the Pain...

When the bewildered classmates realized they were in for a Bruce Willis concert, panic set in and scores of well-dressed alumni were immediately trampled by a frantic, heaving rush to the ballroom doors. Before the mass of humanity was able to push their way out to freedom, a series of loud, thunderous clanks rang through the room and halted the charging mob. The doors in the windowless room were now dead-bolted shut. Within moments, the delirious classmates took cover under tables and cowered in the corners to somehow avoid the bombastic atonal caterwauling, grandiose tough-guy posturing, endless harmonica solos, and non-stop, in-your-face windmilling air guitar.

Willis was oblivious to his one-time friends' visible pain and pleas for mercy. Shouts of "Stop Bruce! You bastard!" and "No more Die Hard movies" were drowned out by deafening choruses of "Ain't Too Proud to Beg" and "Good Lovin'" emanating from the stage. The actor kept gleefully butchering one soul-free blues ditty after another, taking time only to toss Planet Hollywood T-shirts in the crowd (also for sale in the lobby) and to high-five his band mates.

Willis hired a legion of burly, black-clad security guards to make sure everyone stayed in the room and physically forced some of the attendees to applaud by grabbing their lifeless arms and slapping them together.

"I heard stories that people actually went to hear him perform," said Goldman. "But I never believed it. No one did, until now. This is how that bastard fills a room. Trickery! Treachery! What an animal! I could see blood pouring from people's ears and spewing from their twitching mouths. It was like that movie *Carrie*, except the popular guy didn't die."

The unbridled horror climaxed as Bruce — A.K.A Bruno and his Accelerators — were joined on stage for a 32-minute "Soul Man" encore by special celebrity guests and Garden State luminaries including Southside Johnny, Bobby Bandiera, three fat guys who were killed off on *The Sopranos*, Gary U.S. Bonds, Bruce Springsteen's road manager's nephew, Joe Piscopo, Christie Todd Whitman, Kevin Smith's college roommate, Tico Torres, Captain Lou Albano, Brian Seymour, Pat Roddy and Yogi Berra.

After three hours of non-stop sonic torture, the doors sprung open, and paramedics rushed in and started triage on the trampled victims and those who sliced off their ears. Bruce waltzed off stage into a waiting limo and asked his managers how many CDs he had sold.

World's Weakest Man Competition Debuts on New ESPN 3 Channel

Capitalizing on the strength of its popular strongmen competitions, ESPN will kick off its latest cable venture, ESPN 3, with a new high-octane competition show featuring some of the weakest men in the known world battling through a gauntlet of sweat-free, aerobic-free, quasi-athletic tasks. Producers of the show hope to reel in viewers with the series' unique focus on the regular guy and his pathetic lack of physical strength, stamina and courage.

"World's Weakest Man" kicks off this November with the U.S. qualifying rounds held in Philadelphia's Lincoln Financial Field. Here's a sneak peek at some season premiere highlights:

Watch the sweat beads fly as Dallas software developer Tom Jericho goes head-to-head with San Francisco graphic designer Greg Reinhart in the **Blackberry Bench Press Contest**. Each man will test the limits of his spindly, pipe-cleaner arms and hairless, concave chest as he lies on his narrow back and sees who can lower and raise the small, hand-held communications device off their chest the most times. Their "Frak You" and "Byte Me" T-shirts are drenched to the bone as these sedentary soldiers eschew trash-talk, avoid eye-to-eye contact and try their best to pump out some serious reps.

Witness Bala Cynwyd, PA dentist Jonah Levinson barely escape serious injury as he trips over his rake and is almost crushed by the two small handfuls of dry, freshly-fallen sycamore leaves he was attempting to bag in the dizzying, adrenaline-fueled *Lawn Tidying Contest*. Will the wispy warrior's wife lets him return to action after he receives medical treatment for a mildly strained earlobe and a bitten tongue? Tune in and see!

The *Printer Paper Clean, Jerk and Load* Contest pits 130-pound Denver financial consultant Charlie Paulson and 123-lb. NYC record store clerk/bass player Darrel Tarentozzi in a grueling strength and agility match where combatants must lift printer paper (Bright White Lasercopy 2000, 10 sheets at a time) off the ground, raise overhead and then fill the empty, menacing printer tray as quickly as possible. Success is met when the tray is fully loaded and the blinking "Refill Paper Tray" light goes off for good.

Pushing the limits of safety and sanity, two men compete in the perilous *Obstacle-Free Course*. Mickey Morrison, a hedge-fund manager from Chicago, maneuvers his 340 pounds of muscleless flab through a treacherously straight, 10-meter course of evenly paved, impediment-free concrete while pushing a child's toy baby carriage (11 ounces of solid plastic) filled with four packs of Mentos. His competition in this event is Boston-based interior designer DeMarco Carroll. "I haven't been training for weeks," said the enfeebled and unconfident entrant. "I'm also very frightened."

"Don't let these guys fool you, they're ready to rumble," said show producer and retired golfer Craig Preschutto in his best Michael Buffer voice. "They may be out of shape, scared and coughing up blood, but they give 100%... okay maybe 50%, but they do it all for their country! God bless America!"

The new spin-off channel will continue to satiate the action-craving male demographic with a steady diet of sports and competition-based entertainment similar to that offered 24/7 on ESPN, ESPN 2, ESPN Classics and ESPN Shopping Network. New shows and telecasts include: "Co-ed Australian Rules Football," "World Cup Frisbee Golf," "Dump Truck Racing," "Father and Son Backyard Catch," "U.S. Championship Jenga," "Extreme Ocean Water Polo," "National Pinball Playoffs" and "PGA Golf." In addition, ESPN 3 will offer three new reality series: "Rodeo Clown College," "Sports' Sexiest Steroid Abusers" and "Who Wants to Marry an Overweight, Fantasy-Football-Playing Gambling Addict?"

Cell Phone Credited with Dramatic Rise of Jen Finding Something Better to Do

Only a decade ago, a 26-year-old Philadelphia resident like Jen McCaffrey would have found herself stuck in the same bar with the same people for hours at a time, not knowing if people she knew were having a better time somewhere else. This agony of ignorance would have eaten away at the well-connected marketing manager so much that she could not have enjoyed the moment at hand.

That nightmare is over, thanks to a technology revolution enabled by genius, hardwork, millions in infrastructure, and McCaffrey's own persistence.

McCaffrey badgers friends and mere acquaintances relentlessly to keep their cell phones on at all times so she could keep in touch during the night. Her hard work has paid off. She now has over 367 phone numbers of current friends, college friends, high school friends, coworkers, bartenders and door people at trendy clubs and popular bars stored in her phone's address book. Most of these people have abided by McCaffrey's wishes and are only a fully charged flip-phone away.

Being completely aware of what everyone is doing at any given moment is the only thing that gives McCaffrey joy and has led to a major easing of her stress-related, bleeding ulcer. To accomplish this Herculean task of merriment monitoring, McCaffrey is never without her cell phone comfortably resting between her left ear and left hand. If not there, her dark blue Motorola V3x Limited Edition Razr GSM World is being expertly pecked by her trusty right hand with the dexterity of an 80-words-a-minute typist.

From the time she enters a bar, car, restroom or cab, the invaluable vessel of digital communication is being put to use making sure possible fun is not eluding her. Charting her progress at her job with an elaborate spreadsheet (instead of doing work), McCaffrey figured out she's only missed two "blasts," one "raging all-nighter" and three "really hot boys" since her non-stop text and voice barrage has been in full effect.

"Before Jen even has her first cosmo in hand, she's gabbing on that stupid phone, asking in that fake sweet voice, 'Where are you?' always followed up with 'So who's there?'" said Adam Silverstein, one of McCaffrey's frequent bar-hopping companions. "She's so wrapped up in her little gabfest; I usually have to text her from two feet away just to see what she wants from the bar."

While never fully admitting it, McCaffrey is always on a mission to find something better to do. "I just like to be connected and hate missing a good time," said McCaffrey in between calls as she stood outside of Eulogy bar in the trendy Old City section of Philly. "If I wasn't keeping tabs on things for everyone, we would have missed Jamie's killer gig the other night and would have stayed in that lame Irish bar staring at the same bunch of drunk, ugly guys in khakis and baseball hats... yuck!"

Because McCaffrey is the prettiest of her five girlfriends with whom she usually goes out partying, she has no qualms about steering her group away from a perfectly good time in uncertain hopes of meeting different people in a "funner" environment. The group will sometimes complain and put up a minor protest, but never wanting to miss a more enjoyable time themselves, they always jump to attention and join her in the quest for betterment.

"Nothing annoys me more than my friends not having their phones on or charged up. That's why I have six back-up batteries..." McCaffrey stopped to answer her ringing phone, held up her free hand in the "talk to the hand" position directly in front of her companions' faces and walked away to get better reception. Her voice quickly changed from bothered to flirtatious: "What's going on, sweetie?"

"When she does put down the phone at a bar — a very rare occurrence — she just cranes her neck and moves it back and forth like an oscillating fan looking to see who has come in or left," said less-pretty friend Margaret "Mags" Whelan. "Or everyone will be chatting at the table and she'll just be looking down at her lap, manically text messaging someone."

"I love her new move," Adam added with a laugh. He was speaking of McCaffrey's new Bluetooth she has been using of late. This high-tech contraption — normally reserved for the car of office — allows McCaffrey to chat without holding the phone up to her mouth. This also allows for more expressive gesticulation and the ability to hold both a drink and a lit cigarette. "It looks like she's just yapping aloud to herself, pretty freaky. But she's oblivious. One guy came up to her last night because he thought she was talking to him. She just blew him off like Molly Ringwald dismissing Farmer Ted in Sixteen Candles. It was brutal!"

Similar to a person afflicted with OCD who must shut all open doors and cabinets, McCaffrey cannot resist the urge to answer her ringing beacon of connectivity. "Why have it and not use it? Life is too short to have a lame time while a better time is..." The phone rings and she is off again, gleefully conversing through her 10,000-Minutes-a-Month phone plan.

McCaffrey's frequent, abrupt endings of conversations for the sake of the ringer do not surprise her peers anymore. Reports from friends, relatives and coworkers confirm McCaffrey has answered calls while: driving, showering, swimming, moving her bowels, reading at mass, performing oral sex, holding her newborn nephew, skiing, performing CPR and vomiting into a friend's hat.

Spee D'oh!

Whether you're packing a light saber or a light switch, you shouldn't prance about in public donning a Speedo. The skimpy male swimwear has many different names on many different beaches across the globe — each term painting a picture more unsavory than the next. Here's a list of some old favorites and some new gems, some submitted by our readers.

- Marble Sack
- Banana Hammock
- Grape Smuggler
- Australian Dick Sticker
- Nut Hut
- Boner Suit
- Scrote Tote
- Nantucket Nad Bucket
- Sausage Sling
- Portuguese Pud Purse
- Ouch Pouch
- Cock Sock

- Peach Pit Papoose
- Ballbushka
- Lolly Catcher
- Daytona Dong Sarong
- Sperm Tourniquet
- Nugget-Hug-It
- Brazilian Ball Bag
- Manberry Pudding Pack
- Miami Meat Tent
- Saint-Tropez Truffle Duffle
- Bratwurst Bath Cap
- Pickle Pincher

NBC Honors Orbach With New "Law & Order: Briscoe's Best Crime Scene Quips"

After viewing a grossly mangled dead body of a young woman who apparently fell from a balcony six stories above, the late Jerry Orbach's beloved character Det. Lennie Briscoe quickly quipped, "Wonder if her friends knew she was dropping by?"

At another grisly crime scene, Det. Briscoe pulled open a body bag to see a decapitated body of a teenage boy and deadpanned to no one in particular, "Hope his parents weren't getting him any hats for Christmas."

These are just a couple of the morbid bon mots that the weathered old Det. Briscoe regularly dished out on the long running NBC hit "Law & Order." Now there is finally a video collection available capturing over 100 of his greatest callous remarks that have absolutely no regard for the dead or their grieving family members.

"Looks like they lucked out and found the one Chinaman in New York who doesn't know karate," zinged Briscoe after looking over the bloodied body of a Chinese delivery boy who was robbed and beaten to death by a gang of white youths.

Now-deceased actor Orbach once described the genesis of his now famous heartless, abhorrent one-liners, "Most people don't realize it, but I ad lib all of those great lines. In the early days, the scripts were a little staid and too dry, very 'Dragnet.' So I decided to spice things up with some good old fashioned gallows humor."

Orbach perked up and proudly continued, "Some people make jokes to ease the uncomfortable nature of death and murder. I just make jokes because I think death is funny. I love it! I also love that 'Jackass' show and 'Cops,' anything violent cheers me up."

On a rare occasion, you'll find Briscoe mixing in some pop-culture references to appeal to the kids. "Who let the dogs out? Who? Who?" said the recovering alcoholic gumshoe upon seeing the disemboweled body of a female jogger who was the victim of a fatal pit bull attack. When his partner Det. Green failed to acknowledge his tuneful observation, Briscoe continued. "The jogger looks pretty fit, at least the little doggy had a healthy meal."

In a very poignant older episode, Briscoe witnessed the brutal murder of his partner Larry McMurphy (one of 32 that have appeared with him on the show since 1990). As his dying partner whispered his last request for Briscoe to tell his children he loves them, Briscoe cut him off mid-sentence, "Save it for St. Peter, buddy, I got my own problems."

Sam Waterston, who plays District Attorney Jack McCoy, can't wait for the video. "Jerry is a comic genius and one scary mother-effer. He can't stop giggling during all the crime scenes. We have to re-shoot like twenty times before he settles down. My favorite line of Jerry's was when he investigated the bludgeoning of a nun and cracked, 'Hope this doesn't become habit forming.'"

The "Law & Order" franchise is so popular that NBC has three more spin-offs in the works to add to the current lineup of "Law & Order: Special Victims Unit" and "Law & Order: Criminal Intent." Look for the future debuts of "Law & Order: Tactical Truancy Squad," "Law & Order: Roughing Up The Perps" and "Law & Order: FuckFest 2009."

Tonight on Your Local News!

- '30 Rock' to Air an Entire Season of Shows with Guest Stars This Fall, No Regulars, Just Guest Stars!

- Cast From "Extreme Makeover: Home Edition" Sustains Injuries While Patting Themselves on Back

- Americans Lose Gold Medal, World Suspected of Cheating!

- Sarah Jessica Parker Wins Emmy; Celebrates with Delicious Bale of Hay!

- Six Years Later, ESPN Anchor Still Says "Booya!"

- Hilary Swank Looks for More Roles for Women Who Strongly Resemble Men!

- Yankees Sign Michael Phelps, Judd Apatow and Nicholas Sparks to Long-Term, Billion-Dollar Deals!

- Popular Rapper Wins "Best Stabbing" at Recent Awards Show!

- Bush Vows to Unite Divided Nation... Against Gays, Heathens and The Poor!

- Laura Bush Celebrates Victory with Frozen, Vacant Smile!

- Tom Waits to Reprise Scarlett Johansson role in *Lost in Translation* Remake!

- Paris Hilton's Vagina Tires of Limelight, Plans to Move to English Countryside!

- Rachel Ray Discovers $40 a Day Goes Very Far at McDonald's!

- Find Great Mortgage Rates Right in Your Inbox

- Beyonce Tests the Limits of Skin-Tight Pants!

- Kurt Loder Interrupts David Archuleta Interview Sobbing, "Good Lord, What Have I Done with My Life!"

- Travolta Turns Down Bad Role, Opts for Much Worse One!

- Marketing Assistant Adds 132 Instances of Flying and Spinning Multicolored Text to 6-Page PowerPoint Presentation!

- "Joey" Debuts on NBC! "Ross" Debuts in Schwimmer's Dream!

- Bon Jovi's Eyebrows Vow Never to Return to Band!

- Woman Becomes Wine Expert After One Weekend Trip to Napa!

- Cast of "The Real Housewives of Orange County" and Satan Renegotiate Faustian Contract!

- Julia Child Laid to Rest with Side of Potatoes and Sprig of Parsley!

- Teens Eat Up Edible Cell Phones!

- Man Completes Online College Degree During Lunch Break!

- Low-Carb Potatoes Found to Be Hollow!

- Discovery Channel Debuts "American Dent Repair!"

- Lobsters Attacks! Boil Man Alive!

- 'Desperate Housewife' Face Collapses on Set!

- Bush Claims Economy is Rebounding as Magnetic Ribbon Manufacturers Report Record Gains!

Business News

Prosthetics Company Looks Forward to Fourth of July Celebrations

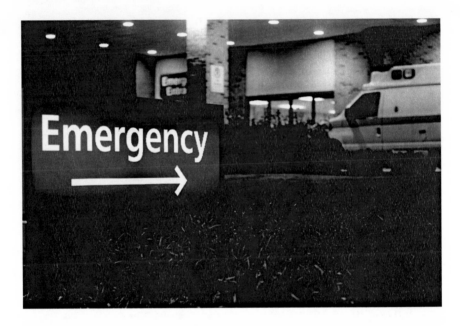

Most sectors of the manufacturing economy are reporting poor results this quarter, but seasonal demand is expected to boost revenues at one enterprising medical devices manufacturer.

"I'm not going out on a limb saying our business explodes during the Fourth of July," said Jerry Dornhoffer, VP of marketing for DornCo Prosthetics International (AMEX: NUTO). He winked and mugged as he continued, "We prepare all year for the burst of business that comes along with firework-based celebrations. Hands down, we are the best at what we do, and it's no accident we're the largest supplier of prosthetics products in the area."

Dornhoffer refers to this patriotic holiday season as his "boom time," where keeping emergency rooms stocked with the latest artificial fingers, hands, arms, legs, ears, noses, and other valuable appendages is his main priority. "This is that golden time of the business year when we acquire a whole new customer base." Asked if by customer base, he meant the unabashedly irresponsible drunken revelers who lose body parts after setting off explosives near their loved ones without taking any safety precautions whatsoever, Dornhoffer replied, "I'm sorry, yes, we call them customers, accident victim is such a negative term, and we try to be customer-friendly here."

Your Loss Is Our Gain reads a sign at the entrance of DornCo world headquarters in Dillon, SC. The rural town of Dillon is also the home of South of the Border, the largest purveyor of fireworks, firecrackers and other limb-loosening entertainment products in the United States. "It's no coincidence that we are conveniently located in the same town and on the same street as SOB," continued Dornhoffer as he walked us through his building and gave a tour of the high-tech labs. "Throughout the year we work in conjunction with our friends at SOB and glean invaluable information from their latest technological advances. That way we can be prepared for the latest accidents and develop our products accordingly. It really sparks our imagination. You gotta love the synergy!"

"The old Scuddy Buddy M-80s used to only blow off one, two fingers tops, and the fingers were still 'live' as we say in the industry — meaning they could be re-attached, not good for a replacement parts business like DornCo. Now, thanks to the fellas at SOB, the new Ultra M-200s are guaranteed to blow three to four digits clean off and reduce them to unrecoverable ashes! This is fantastic news for us!"

DornCo does most of his business with hospitals in rural areas where drinking and the lighting of life-threatening combustible party enhancers go together.

"DornCo is fabulous. They always make sure we have dozens of varieties of prosthetic limbs and appendages available in all the latest styles and colors," said Dr. Marianne Brace Grayson of Sacred Heart Hospital in Scottsburg, IN.

"DornCo's products are the essence of accessible design for the newly disabled, who generally want to continue their old habits with as little disruption as possible. DornCo's artificial limbs help by containing compartments and pockets that can hold firecrackers, bottle rockets, mini Roman candles and most importantly, matches."

When asked if this sort of modification was an unethical attempt to gain repeat business through additional injuries, Dr. Grayson replied, "Managed health care has hit us all hard. No further comment."

"I guess you could call us a true 'hands-free technology,'" laughed Dornhoffer as he picks up a few of his latest hand-to-forearm models and performs some karate moves accented by some verbal "hi-yahs!" in a bad Chinese accent. "We really have fun here and take pride in our work knowing we provide a great service to people whose partying gets a little out of hand."

"I know this one fella who lost a hand, a foot, his nose, and both ears when his buddy lit a can of firecrackers off under his folding chair," said Dornhoffer "Sure, it sounds like fun and everyone loves a good prank, but for those times when your toes end up in the punchbowl and are charred beyond recognition, DornCo has some new piggies ready and waiting for you at your local ER."

The prostheses are also low priced compared to other similar products in the market. "We realize the majority of our customers don't have insurance. They don't want to pay a lot for their body parts, and many can't afford to keep purchasing new ones. That's why we don't want to charge them an arm and..." Dornhoffer starts to laugh and tries to regain composure, "... and arm and a leg! Sorry, but that never gets old!"

Like most successful companies, customer satisfaction is DornCo's main concern. "We always get a thumbs up from all are customers... well, right after they've been re-attached!"

Photo Agencies Report Record Sales of "Distressed Businessman" Images

While the majority of large businesses and corporations are feeling the crushing pain of the nation's economic woes, photos agencies like Getty, Reuters, Associated Press and others are doing bang-up business in one particular category.

"Over the past couple of weeks demand has been overwhelming. Newspapers and websites need at least 10 to 20 photos a day of traders, bankers and other Wall Street types seriously losing their shit. We got a ton of these misery shots, so it's pretty awesome for us," said Jake Deponcere.

According to Deponcere, most searches are for: "Stock Ticker" AND "Angry Trader" AND "Clenched Fist" OR "Hands on Sad Face." Other popular search terms and phrases are: "Screaming Banker," "Utterly Despondent Businessman" and "Hopeless Guy with Loosened Tie Staring at Record Low Financial Numbers on Multiple Monitors."

According to most news editors, these photos are necessary and they will pay top dollar for them because "even with the economy completely fucked, people love seeing these Wall Street douchebags totally eat it."

Daniel Day-Lewis Kills Man to Prepare for Role

"Correct me if I am wrong, but I am almost certain Tony Hopkins did *not* actually bite into the sweet flesh of a screaming human being when he portrayed that saucy roué Hannibal Lecter, now did he?" said brooding British method actor Daniel Day-Lewis, speaking on the set of his new movie *City of Butcherly Love*. "Tony's a decent bloke, but a complete fraud of an actor."

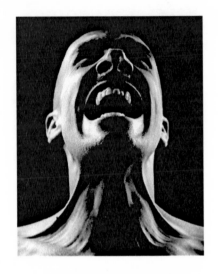

Day-Lewis, renowned for his intense style of acting, starts prepping for his roles months in advance and takes on the character's persona for the entire time. According to Day-Lewis, "A good method man never turns it off."

Method acting can be described as a naturalistic style of acting made famous by the Russian actor-director, Konstantin Stanislavsky, where the actor identifies closely with the character to be portrayed. Marlon Brando started the method ball rolling in the U.S. with his highly emotional performance in *On The Waterfront*. Brando is now famous for becoming his character prior to filming. The planned capstone for his career was to play his role as the mentally ill, obese, 14th-century Italian opera singer Enrico Lozengia. For more than 30 years he refused to begin production until he has reached the singer's true weight of 900 pounds. He died only thirty pounds away from his goal.

A Madness to His Method

For his role of Christy Brown in the 1989 film *My Left Foot*, Day-Lewis had both his arms and one leg broken so he could truly feel what it is like to be a physically disabled. He also kept a live chipmunk in his cheek to disrupt his normal speech pattern and to produce the sound of a man who had to struggle to speak.

Day-Lewis trained for a whole year in the ring and sparred daily with professional middleweight boxers to prep for his critically acclaimed lead role in the 1997 drama *The Boxer*. The thespian pugilist embraced the sweet science so much he recently went on a celebrity boxing tour (sponsored by PBS) and defeated the likes of Mickey Rourke, Will Smith and Dustin Diamond.

In keeping with his strange yet effective preparation, Lewis donned a giant black top hat for five months straight for his role as the ultra-violent Bill "The Butcher" Cutting in the Martin Scorsese film *Gangs of New York*. He did not take off the towering topper even for his weekly shower. Day-Lewis described the headpiece as "a part of me. It gave me strength and fearlessness... plus I could hide my favorite large killing-axe in it."

"Mr. Day-Lewis would not allow anyone — cast or crew members — to speak directly to him. We had to address his hat," said production assistant Mitch Keady. "It was a bit weird, but he is so fantastic we didn't care!"

A Most Unsettling Set

In what many are calling the greatest achievement in method acting to date, Day-Lewis murdered a homeless man to immerse himself in his latest role as a serial killer roaming the streets of Philadelphia. With the cameras rolling on a closed set in North Philly, a withered old homeless man was tricked into entering a decrepit warehouse door that read "Free Food and Parkas!" Once inside, the frail man was tackled by three burly gaffers and a best boy and immediately injected with a large dose of Phenobarbital and some A-1 steak sauce.

Then, suddenly, a naked and feral Day-Lewis pounced into the darkened room and quickly mauled the man to death. Biting, scratching, shredding, screaming, ululating like the alpha wolf partaking in a fresh kill, Lewis became the character. Seconds later, it was over and the stunned crew burst into applause. The actor was subdued with a dart gun and put back into his cage.

"It had to be done. How could I honestly portray a murderous sociopath if I had never experienced the act of brutal, bloody murder? Okay, well, maybe once in college... but that was long ago," said Day-Lewis hours after his heinous rampage.

In a deal brokered with the Philadelphia Film Commission, the producers of the movie and the Philadelphia Police Department, Lewis will not be brought up on any criminal charges. "With all the money and jobs City of Butcherly Love is bringing to our town, one little murder is a small price to pay," said Karen Reddman, head of the Film Commission. "This is a high-profile movie. When Hollywood producers hear how accommodating Philly is, they will think of us when they're scouting for their next project. It's great P.R.!"

When filming commences, Day-Lewis will retreat to Hawaii for a grueling six-month crash course in surfing to ready himself for his part in the upcoming Miley Cyrus sun-n-surf musical *Gidget Meets Gidget*.

Free Band Names!

- **Try This at Home** - taken by band from the UK.

- **Terror Tapes** - taken by indie alt band from Maryland.

- **All Right Hamilton** - taken by band from Cape Town, SA.

- **Today's Top Stories** - taken by a band in Little Rock, AR.

- **Not What It Looks Like** - taken by Callum.

- **Hard-Fought Hugs** - taken by Alex from Ohio.

- **Shapeshifting for Beginners** - taken by Nathan.

- **The Record Lows** - taken by pop-punk Band from New York.

- **The Button Pushers** - taken by indie pop alternative band from UK.

- **Belligerent Design**- taken by three headbangers from WV.

- **Newcastle Coal Shoot** - taken by an emo and rock band from CA.

- **Girly-Drink Drunks** - taken by pop rock all girl band from WA.

- **Ghosts with Vampire Accents** - taken by a indie band out of Dallas.

- **We Need to Talk** - taken by a soul/rock band from Australia.

Life

My Fun Dad

As I'm about to experience Father's Day as a father, please allow me to talk about "Dad." Don't worry, I'm not about to traipse over the cutesy, sleep-deprived, new-dad territory that so many have traveled on before.

I'm sure my experience is no different than most new fathers (except that my daughter rules!): wonderfully satisfying, weepingly joyous and at times, extremely scary. Instead, I'd just like to tell you about my dad, Donald P. Lyons (AKA "Big D"), and the various ways he made me laugh like hell throughout my life.

Picasso — When I was a baby, my Mom and Dad decided to move from North Jersey to the beach — Belmar, NJ, to be specific. In preparation, my dad decided to paint the house to make it more appealing and didn't let his complete lack of painting experience and limited artistic skill get in his way. After the job was hastily completed, my uncle said a good lawn mowing would also be wise due to the 10- to 12-inch-high grass that covered our yard. Once the grass was mowed, it was quite apparent where the new paint ended — about a foot above the ground — leaving a sizable grass-shaped swath of old paint along the entire perimeter of the house. Live and learn. Speaking of paint, my dad once painted his brother Bill's car while he was away in the service. It would have been better appreciated if he didn't use oil-based house paint.

Fun Machine — In a very "Homer" moment (and I'm not talking about the early Greek poet) while our young family was Christmas shopping at the Seaview Square Mall, Dad was stopped in his tracks by a man playing a colorful keyboard with the greatest of ease in front of a music store. This was no ordinary organ. It was a grand concert of splendiferous sound emanating from a machine the size of a small upright piano. Built with the best technology the 1970s had to offer, this electronic melody-maker sounded like a whole orchestra replete with horns, brass, woodwinds and a killer rhythm section that played a wide variety of styles from the rumba to rock. With little to no piano playing experience, anyone could learn to play in just a couple hours and be the hit of the party! Or so the pitch went. It was quite awesome.

When we noticed the price tag was $1,200, we laughed knowing it was so ridiculously out of our price range (a bag of kazoos was a bit more realistic). We went on our way. Except for Don. who lingered a bit with a dreamy smile on his face as if he was in some sort of trance. Don liked music and Don liked parties.

I'm not saying we didn't have a lot of money at the time, but a plastic pinball machine, two worn green vinyl couches, a large plastic palm tree and an entertainment unit built from cinder blocks and black spray-painted planks of wood were the highlights of our living room. So you would imagine my great surprise when my mom, brother D.J. and I discovered the wildly expensive "Fun Machine" — which costs about three times as much as the family car — was sitting next to the tree on Christmas morning. I don't know how Donnie pulled it off and at the time, nor did I care! This thing ruled. We all went nuts. My dad was so proud.

A tale like this would usually end with the expensive impulse purchase being ignored as soon as we got bored with it. It would then gather dust in the garage (next to my old LiteBrite with the word "FART" colorfully displayed on it), its faux ivories never to be tickled again. Everyone would laugh at Don and his rash purchase.

But no! The machine provided maximum merriment and was the hit of our parties for a solid ten years, with slightly sauced friends and family clamoring to take the helm and bust out some "Wait Til the Sun Shines Nelly" and "I'm Just Wild About Harry" sing-a-longs into the wee hours. Uncle Nick and his rendition of "Blue Hawaii" led the charge. The good ol' Fun Machine still sits in our side room, entertaining my daughter, niece, and visiting toddlers from time to time. Sure, Don could have been practical and used the money for D.J.'s asthma medicine or new windows that squirrels couldn't scamper through, but where would the fun be in that?

Pleather Jacket — So you get the idea that we weren't the Rockefellers, but we always got by and my pops would do his best to keep within our limited budget set up by my mom. My dad was a smart guy, a financial adviser, so despite some whimsical purchases, he knew the value of a dollar. Case in point, he bought a caramel-colored, fake-leather driving jacket for six bucks at the local Two Guys (a budget Wal-Mart) in Neptune City. Six bucks! The new Sweet album (Desolation Boulevard) D.J. and I saved for and purchased the same day cost more. The poorly tailored piece of pleather was about as stiff and thick as a sheet of cardboard and Donnie wore the thing proudly for at least five years. before he became a fledgling member of the Members Only jacket club. He earned his epaulets.

Cement Court — My dad wasn't the most handy fella in the world. While his brothers and other male relatives built impressive decks, additions and other manly creations, Big D was most comfortable using black electrical tape to remedy most repair jobs. He did not have a tool box, keeping his vast array of old screwdrivers and wrenches in a drawer in the kitchen instead. Some other tools could be found in the grass in the backyard for safe keeping. Anyway, after successfully putting up a backboard on our garage with the help of Uncle Frank (no Bob Villa himself), we all immediately noticed that dribbling a basketball on the bumpy grass below would be pretty darn lame.

"Hey, let's play some b-ball at D.J. and Jeff's house! They have this cool grass court with all these sharp, rusted tools you need to dodge while driving to the basket! It's insanely dangerous and fun!"

After assessing the problem, my dad decided he would build a cement court himself. Knowing even less about masonry than painting, my dad bought about 10 giant bags of ready-mix cement, masonry tools and a bunch of two-by-fours to frame out our new massive court. After two full days of blood, sweat and toil and using up all the bags and his all his energy, he took a step back to behold the fruits of his labor: a sad, three-foot by three-foot piece of thin, uneven cement about 12 feet from the basket. "Geez, we might need a few more bags!" chuckled Don.

But we didn't need more bags. Donnie needed to rest and to catch the end of a Mets doubleheader. The court was not finished that summer or any summer after. Occasionally, years later, when we were all in the back yard, D.J. and I would pretend to have a one-on-one game solely contained on the small patch of cement. My dad would laugh and gives us that "What the hell was I thinking" look. I loved that look.

Communion Photo — In sixth grade I had to write an autobiography for a class project. I gave it to my Mom and Dad to proof and they were a bit embarrassed by one of the photos I included. The photo showed me sitting on our front porch in a little blue denim leisure-style suit (which was fabulous), opening some gifts I received for my first holy communion. They weren't embarrassed of my goofy mug (this time), but were aghast at the condition of the front porch. The porch was black, but many of the planks showed off bare wood and chipped paint. It was in desperate need of a new coat or two. Instead of being inspired to go paint the porch (which was probably still in the same condition four years later), my dad simply took out a black pen and colored in all the bare wood in the photo. Don then handed me the booklet, "Good as new!" Who needs Photoshop when you have a Bic?

Coffee — My wonderful mother Patricia was a nurse and worked most Saturdays when we were young, so Don took care of my brother and I. Saturdays were pretty busy and my dad needed to get us ready for our early soccer games. As I mentioned earlier, the windows in our house were old and drafty and let in their fair share of November coldness, so the mornings were a tad chilly at Chez Lyons. In an attempt to warm up 7-year-old D.J. and 6-year-old Jeff, Don gave us the warmest thing handy — a piping hot cup of coffee. No matter how much sugar or milk I put in it, I just couldn't down it. D.J., on the other hand, took to the delicious hot caffeinated beverage like a ravenous lion eating a freshly killed gazelle. The majority of pediatricians might differ, but Don's cure-all for coldness worked extremely well. D.J. was the warmest, fastest, most energetic kid on the field every Saturday. And well into Sunday.

Coaching Soccer — Speaking of soccer, my dad was a successful soccer coach. When Belmar was in need of soccer coaches, they asked my dad, who already coached baseball and basketball for the town's recreation department, to lend a hand. My dad was a good athlete who loved baseball (he pitched a no-hitter in high school), so coaching another sport seemed easy enough. When Don was growing up in Newark, NJ, soccer was not the most popular sport. "Sissies in shorts who kick each other," was how it was referred to by most. Not letting his ignorance of the game stop him, Don went to the library and perused a few books on the game. He was good to go. His style of coaching was unique. He found the best player on the team, 9-year-old George Parker, and pretty much let him run things, telling Don where everyone should play. Don just stood on the sidelines and yelled, "Go get 'em guys" and other words of encouragement. We came in first three years in a row.

Naps -— Living at the shore, we'd have lots of company pop in all the time. This did not preclude Don from taking his beloved eye-closers when he deemed necessary. With a front porch teeming with friends and relatives from North Jersey and beyond, Don would excuse himself from his wicker chair and enter the house. After about an hour or so, some one might ask, "Where'd Don go? I thought he was getting me a beer." But most knew where Don went and didn't bother to ask. He'd reappear an hour or two later, refreshed and ready to enjoy the parade of people marching by the house.

German Beer — My dad was a Budweiser drinker. Once, when I came home from college with some friends, Don took me aside and said, "Hey, I was in the liquor store and I saw some German beer that was on sale so I got a couple cases for you and the guys." He was very impressed with his purchase, as was I.. until I opened the fridge and saw two cases of Meister Brau with bright orange $7.99 price stickers. We drank the budget domestic beer and thanked Don repeatedly for the treat. He didn't touch the stuff.

Hitting the Boards — Some of my pals — Gowen, Yaz, Demarcs, Hewson, B.C. — were lifeguards in Spring Lake. My dad liked to jog the boardwalk in the town and yell out "Hi guys!" to the guards as he approached their stands early in the morning. The guards would look over their left shoulders, say "Hey Mr. Lyons" and turn back to staring at the ocean. 10 to 15 minutes later, they'd look over their right shoulder and see my dad only about 20 yards further down the boards from where they last spotted him. Don was the slowest runner in the history of human mobility. "You gotta pace yourself," he would say half joking. I think he just liked to suck in the scenery. He always stayed a safe distance away from the rat race.

Driving Mr. Ziggy — For the majority of my life, we did not have the luxury of air conditioning. So the family spent a lot of time outside in the summer, except for our dog. Ziggy was an overweight beagle that was a bit difficult — not very affectionate, bad gas — and did not handle the heat well. The dog only really liked Don, and Don really loved that dog. When the heat would get into the 90s, my dad would load Zig into the car and drive around aimlessly just so the paunchy pup could enjoy the blasting A.C. in his face. That's love.

Sadly, my dad died suddenly in 1996 at the age of 61. Nothing can prepare you for losing a loved one, especially a wonderful father who brought so much joy to all in his humble, low-key manner. The last time I saw him he was standing on the porch with Patty smiling and waving good bye to my friends and I as we drove off after a day of canoeing and barbequing at the shore. I remember thinking, "Man, what a cute couple."

I still miss him terribly, but retelling tales again and again helps me deal and keeps him close to me. Don Lyons was a normal guy with a great sense of humor who loved the Mets, the beach, Ireland, singing aloud and just taking care of his wife and boys. He was the best father a fella could have. So here's to my dear old Dad, thanks pal! And to all my friends — D.J., Brian, Russ, B.C., Mike C., Nies, Parker, Williams, Linda — whose dads passed away much too early, keep rehashing the good times. The stories never get old.

Used Wigs

Need more nonsense?

Vist:

www.usedwigs.com

www.usedwigsradio.com

CPSIA information can be obtained at www.ICGtesting.com
Printed in the USA
LVOW131936080512

280882LV00002B/189/P